500
TIPS FOR
TEACHERS

**SALLY BROWN, CAROLYN EARLAM
AND PHIL RACE**

**KOGAN
PAGE**

To all the teachers who have helped us with this book, and who are our good friends.

First published in 1995
Reprinted 1996 and 1997

Apart from any fair dealing for the purposes of research or private study, or criticism or review, as permitted under the Copyright, Designs and Patents Act, 1988, this publication may only be reproduced, stored or transmitted, in any form or by any means, with the prior permission in writing of the publishers, or in the case of reprographic reproduction in accordance with the terms of licences issued by the Copyright Licensing Agency. Enquiries concerning reproduction outside those terms should be sent to the publishers at the undermentioned address:

Kogan Page Limited
120 Pentonville Road
London N1 9JN

© Sally Brown, Carolyn Earlam and Phil Race, 1995

British Library Cataloguing in Publication Data

A CIP record for this book is available from the British Library

ISBN 0 7494 1417 0

Typeset by Saxon Graphics Ltd, Derby
Printed and bound in Great Britain by Biddles Ltd, Guildford and King's Lynn

Contents

Introduction

This book is designed to be a useful compendium of sound and practical ideas to help classroom teachers do the job to the best of their ability, particularly but not exclusively those who are new to the profession. It is primarily aimed at secondary school teachers, although those who work with younger children may find elements of the book helpful, while many of the tips are also transferable to further and higher education. First, we would like to set out a few guiding principles on which this book is based:

THIS BOOK SHOULD NOT BE READ COVER TO COVER!

The book is designed to be dipped into, with readers selecting those areas that are of most interest to them. We have assembled 52 sets of ten tips, each of which is intended to be relatively complete in itself. We have grouped the sets under six main headings, although sometimes these divisions have been rather arbitrary, with some sets perfectly capable of being sited in two or more categories. However, as this is a book for grazing on rather than devouring whole, we don't consider that problematic.

THE NEED FOR REAL TRAINING

We believe that there is no substitute for effective teacher training through established courses. This book is designed to be a handy supplement, providing a few tips and wrinkles gleaned from our experience as teachers over many years. All our ideas are offered as part of an à la carte menu; select those elements that are useful to you at the stage you are at now.

THE BASIS OF THIS BOOK

All three of the authors have experience of teaching in secondary schools (as well as many other types of teaching environments) over the last 25 years. Between us we also have extensive experience of teaching in a very wide range of educational establishments in the UK and abroad. We have also between us assessed, moderated, evaluated, validated, acted as consultants, reviewed, written and advised in all kinds of educational contexts.

Part 1 Techniques for effective teaching and classroom management

This section contains advice on some basic techniques of teaching, particularly on interaction with pupils. This is perhaps one of the most difficult areas on which to give advice, because the way we work with children tends to be a very personal thing. Techniques that work with one teacher are completely useless to another, and it is really important to develop your own style that you feel comfortable with. People tend to talk about 'natural authority' as though it were something that one is either born with or not, but in reality everyone has good days and bad days. The principal advantages in being an experienced teacher are that you have learned not to take unpleasant experience too seriously, and that you can learn from mistakes.

We also include here some very practical tips on teaching techniques:

1 Meeting a class for the first time
2 Gaining attention and settling a class down
3 Coping with interruptions
4 Learning names
5 Avoiding disruption in your class
6 Using blackboards
7 Organizing practical lessons
8 Doing yard/bus/break duties painlessly
9 Ensuring equality of opportunity within your teaching

PART 2 PLANNING AND ASSESSMENT

Assessment is a really crucial area of any teacher's work and one that can have a key influence over the ways in which pupils develop and improve. We too are subject to assessment ourselves from time to time, formally through inspection and less formally but equally importantly when we get feedback on our work from our pupils. Much has been written on assessment in schools that we do not intend to replicate here: instead we offer a few suggestions on how to cope with what many teachers see as the most arduous chore of our professional lives!

10 Assessing pupils' work
11 Giving pupils face-to-face feedback
12 Getting feedback from pupils
13 Using self- and peer-assessment
14 Making sense of GNVQ
15 Planning schemes of work

16   Invigilating internal exams
17   Writing reports
18   Preparing for an inspection

Part 3   Using Teaching and Learning Resources Well

The resources we use for our teaching are a crucial element in influencing the quality of our teaching. Outstandingly good teaching materials are not a copper-bottomed guarantee of good teaching, but they do tend to improve the teacher's confidence and they tend to be an area of work that pupils comment on, whether adversely or with praise. Most teachers recognize too that the ways in which resources are used makes all the difference, and that planning of activities is crucial to their success. Here we provide some guidance on the preparation and use of teaching and learning materials to support effective teaching.

19   Preparing interesting handout materials
20   Preparing learning packages
21   Using videos in the classroom
22   Getting the most from the library
23   Organizing resources
24   Making do with limited resources
25   Making your classroom into an attractive learning environment
26   Making effective displays
27   Taking pupils on a trip
28   Visiting museums and art galleries

Part 4   Supporting Pupils' Learning

Helping pupils to learn is what our job is all about. All too often the emphasis is on what is taught rather than what is learned, and this is exacerbated by an excessive emphasis on syllabuses and curriculum matters. Our experience has led us to believe that study skills are less effective when they are provided as an additional 'bolt on' element of class-work. Instead we would argue that it is the job of teachers at all levels to think as much about how pupils are learning as about the content delivered. For this reason, the next section concentrates on how the teacher can help pupils to become more effective learners.

29   Helping pupils who don't read well
30   Helping pupils who don't do maths well
31   Helping pupils to learn together
32   Helping pupils revise effectively
33   Helping pupils to pass exams

Part 5 Providing personal and pastoral care

The teacher's job does not finish when the end-of-lesson bell rings. For many, the pastoral elements of our work tend to be some of the most satisfying and rewarding aspects of our jobs. At the same time, however, they can be problematic, demanding and exhausting. Sometimes we do not know where to start with pastoral matters and often we do not know where to finish. This section aims to give some guidance on some of the most common issues teachers often have to deal with when working on a personal level with children, not only concerned with traumas, but also with the more satisfying task of helping students with preparations for the next phase of their lives.

Part 6 Being an effective colleague

A commonly overheard remark in the staff room is 'I can cope with the kids, it's the other teachers who are driving me up the wall!' This final short section offers some advice on how to work effectively with fellow professionals within the school, how to take care of yourself, and some thoughts on looking to your own future prospects.

CONCLUSIONS

We hope that these suggestions will be useful to you in your teaching career. You may well feel that your experiences put you in a position where you too have advice to give to other teachers. If so, we will be delighted to hear from you, and may well (with your permission) include your ideas, properly credited, in the next edition of this volume.

ACKNOWLEDGEMENTS

Thanks are due to everyone who gave us most constructive advice and criticism at the pilot stage of this book, especially: Tom Carr, Diana Le Cornu, Myles Easterby, Mary Evans, Diane Green, Andrea Heron, Helen Horne, Pat Kenrick, Rob Merville, Geoff Myers, Ken Onions and Denise Whiting.

Sally Brown: *Educational Development Adviser, EDS, University of Northumbria at Newcastle.*

Carolyn Earlam: *Inspector for Art and Design, Durham County Council Education Department.*

Phil Race: *Professor of Educational Development, University of Glamorgan.*

November 1994

Part 1 Techniques for Effective Teaching and Classroom Management

1

Meeting a class for the first time

There is no second chance to make a good first impression! First impressions are crucial in any work with people and none more so than with new pupils. The old adage 'don't smile until Christmas' held a grain of truth – it's always easier to loosen up later than it is to start to lay down the law once your class has decided you're soft!

1 **Don't forget to introduce yourself** – and spell your name out on the blackboard if necessary.

2 **State clearly what you expect of your pupils** – what they can and cannot do in the classroom. Establish a few simple rules of behaviour and always stick to them. You may also wish to invite from pupils their own suggestions for additional ground-rules.

3 **Learn your pupils' names as quickly as you can** – any instruction is much more effective if directed to an individual. Your work will also be more effective if you never forget that your class is made up of individuals, and know them as such.

4 **Help pupils to learn each others' names** if they don't know them already. One way of doing this is to form them into a large circle, and ask each pupil to say (for example) 'my name is Cheryl, and this is my friend Mark, and this is Clive, and . . .' seeing who can say the most names. This helps you learn their names too!

5 **Help pupils to get to know each other** (at the same time helping you to get to know them). For example, conduct a class round along the lines of 'My name is Jean, my favourite thing in the world is pizza, and my pet hate is spiders'.

6 Give your pupils a clear idea of **what they will be doing** in the next few weeks and why they are doing it. Help them to see how your work with them fits in with the syllabus, National Curriculum programmes of study and so on.

7   **Make sure your pupils know how they will be assessed.** Which pieces of work are more important for assessment, which areas are revision of material they have already covered? Emphasize the need for them to look after their own work and take responsibility for their own progress, especially where there is continuous assessment.

8   Use the first lessons to **find out what pupils already know** about the subject and build on this in your planning. You could make this into a quiz or get them to write something which is personal to them which will help you get to know them.

9   **Explain which resources are available for pupils to use;** which they can access themselves and which resources are to be obtained from the teacher, or in the library or resource centre. Encourage pupils to take responsibility for the resources in their classroom, for example keeping an eye on the number of rulers, rubbers, and so on, ensuring that the stock lasts all year.

10   In the first few weeks, **react firmly if any of your rules of behaviour are transgressed.** Show the class that you notice everything that is going on and are not willing to ignore anything. Name the pupil who has done something you don't like, but be aware of individual personalities and notice if what you say is having an extreme effect on anyone. You may need to tread carefully with pupils who feel insecure or nervous. Don't be drawn into arguments; when you know pupils better you can be more flexible.

2

Gaining attention and settling a class down

Nice as it would be if all pupils were sitting quietly, ready to learn and attentive at all times, this is not the nature of the young of the human species! Here are some tips to overcome human nature – but remember that different things work for different people, so find your own styles.

1 **Try doing nothing first.** Stand there, very still, absolutely quiet. The pupils closest will notice, and the word will gradually spread. Give it a moment or two before you decide that another tactic is needed!

2 **Don't shout (yet)!** If all is not quiet, avoid the instinct to shout 'be quiet' at the top of your voice! Start a quiet conversation with two or three pupils who already look ready to listen to you.

3 **Take advantage of human curiosity.** It sometimes pays to whisper! Human nature includes not wishing to miss anything. Whisper to those closest to you, and many of the rest will stop talking and listen.

4 **Drop a non-attender in it!** Ask a question to those who are already listening, but end with the name of someone you know has not been paying attention. Watch, as all eyes turn to this pupil, the effect of someone being found out by their peers not to have been listening.

5 **Have ways of making pupils listen.** Start with something that needs careful listening – for example a tape-recording or video played back quite quietly.

6 **People love praise.** Praise those who are paying attention, particularly if they don't do so normally, rather than grumbling at those pupils who are not yet paying attention.

7 **Begin with a task.** Start a session with something for pupils to do. Have printed instructions on handout materials, or write them on the blackboard in advance.

8 **Select some targets.** Pick on some 'known' live-wires in the class by name, giving them particular tasks to do at the start of a lesson, as leaders of groups of pupils.

9 **Don't take chaos as a personal affront.** Don't regard initial chaos as disrespect to you. Regard it as human nature, and natural until something interesting comes up.

10 **Few want to be left out of some fun!** If you can do this (we're not good at it!) start a lesson by very quietly saying something really amusing to those who have already 'settled down'. The rest will soon become eager to be included in this.

3

Coping with interruptions

'If only I could just get on with my teaching!' – how often have we thought this. When we're interrupted, it's natural to feel emotions including anger and frustration. However, at these times, all eyes tend to be on us – not least to see how we react. The following suggestions may help you deal with interruptions with dignity.

1 **Accept that you are in fact being interrupted.** Trying to carry on as though the source of the interruption were unnoticed tends to do more harm than good, as most pupils will probably be concentrating on the interruption and how you react, rather than on what you had been saying or doing just before the event.

2 **Keep track of where you were.** Make a mental note of exactly what you were doing just before an interruption, so that when you have dealt with it, you can pick up the threads without having to say 'now, where was I?' Also, check whether there are connections between things you do and the probability of interruptions.

3 **Accept that some interruptions will be important and necessary.** When this is so, make sure that anyone responsible for the interruption is not criticized or made to feel embarrassed.

4 **Be patient with colleagues.** Be particularly careful when interrupted by a colleague or other member of staff. Even if the interruption is unwelcome and unnecessary, it is best to have a quiet word with the person concerned later, rather than let any frustration be noticed by your pupils.

5 **Turn interruptions into positive learning experiences.** When possible, draw useful learning points from interruptions by pupils. The more they feel that their interruptions are taken notice of, the more likely they are to avoid making unnecessary ones.

6 **Keep individual feelings for individuals.** When a particular pupil is making too many interruptions, try to have a private word later, rather than a public show of annoyance.

7 **Have something to do ready for anyone who interrupts.** Have a list of relevant questions about the topic of the day, so that anyone who interrupts can be put on the spot if necessary with a question to answer. This can work well at discouraging interruptions!

8 **Watch your distance.** Move up closer to anyone who has made an unwelcome interruption. Pupils are much less brave when you're standing over them than when you're at the other end of the room.

9 **Look for the causes of interruptions.** If there are frequent interruptions, it could be that pupils are tired of listening, and need to be given something definite to get on with. Avoid the 'I've started, so I'll finish' approach.

10 **Learn from colleagues.** When you have the chance, observe how colleagues cope with interruptions. The more techniques you have at your disposal, the more versatile your approach becomes.

4

Learning names

You will know yourself how irritating it is when people forget your name. Calling someone by name makes any message you wish to communicate all the stronger and more personal. However, we often seem to have a whole bunch of new names to tackle at once: the following suggestions may help you with this task.There will always be some names that are very hard to remember, but it's worth making the effort: you may be the only person who does learn such names.

1 **Let pupils decide their names!** Ask your pupils to tell you the the version of their name they wish to be known by and attempt to call them by it unless it is too daft for you to cope with. Michael might hate being called Mick, but Salim might prefer Sal.

2 **Be careful with nicknames.** Be cautious about using a nickname that seems innocuous enough to us, but causes the class to fall about hysterically every time you use it. It may well be that you are unwittingly being drawn into using a vulgar expression unknown to you!

3 **Address questions to named pupils.** To help you to get to know some names, choose people from the class list to answer (easy) questions and bit by bit memorize the respondents' names.

4 **Make a map of the names.** Use a seating plan to note names of pupils against the places where they are sitting and try to encourage them to sit there for the first few lessons until you are more familiar with the class.

5 **Once you've got them, use them.** Once you know some names, use them every time you speak to those pupils (without letting them feel they are being picked on!)

6 **Make names visual.** Some pupils will be happy to wear name labels for the first few days of a session, or you could use folded cardboard name labels on the desk: remember to get them to write their names in really large letters.

7   **One step at a time!** Concentrate on first names for the first part of the school year, and pick up the surnames as you go on.

8   **Take care with the repetitions.** Find out any pupils who share a first name and learn these first. Once you have learned the three Matthews, two Traceys and four Alis you have made a good start!

9   **Make sure you have their names right.** Check you are using the correct names for pupils and encourage them to correct you if you get them wrong. Also check how to pronounce unfamiliar names. It's dreadful to find out at the end of the year that you have been getting one wrong from the beginning.

10 **Be persistent.** Don't expect to learn all the names all at once: build up gradually over the weeks. Don't be too hard on yourself if you never master all of the names, especially if you teach lots of different groups. But do your best: pupils do tend to be critical of teachers who don't make an effort to learn names.

5

Avoiding disruption in your class

This is an area a great deal easier to write about than to follow through – but we all keep battling against the unpredictability of the human factor!

1 **Establish a few clear rules for behaviour in your class.** If possible involve the pupils in the development of these rules. The more ownership you can allow them to feel regarding the rules, the more likely they are to at least try to follow them.

2 **Reward good behaviour immediately with positive feedback** – a smile or a few words of praise or encouragement. Try also to ensure that you are quick to reward the good behaviour of any pupils who are often guilty of bad behaviour – they may really respond to some positive feedback.

3 **Deal with any misdemeanours before they become major incidents.** Often, it is best to deal with minor incidents as privately as you can. Public confrontations arouse too much interest!

4 **Establish what the sanctions will be for transgressing the rules.** Ensure that such sanctions are reasonable and practicable.

5 **Avoid unreasonable expectations of pupils – but don't demean them either.** Ensure that the level of the work you set is suitable for all the individuals within the group, and that pupils experiencing difficulties have manageable targets. Direct the emphasis of your comments towards the work or lack of it. This involves getting to know what each pupil is capable of, and setting realistic targets.

6 **Look for signals.** Be adaptable – change the pace or content of a lesson as soon as you realise it is not working well. Changing approach on the basis of feedback you receive is a strength, not a weakness!

7 **If a particular pupil is causing problems,** immediately remove this pupil to another part of the room. This is a way of demonstrating that you have observed the problem, and also provides such a pupil with the opportunity to start afresh.

8 **Provide 'cooling-off' time.** If you – or a pupil – lose your tempers, try to allow a few minutes for you both to calm down – take the pupil involved out from the room for a short while. It can pave the way towards progress to say something along the lines 'I'm sorry this happened. How can we make sure that this sort of thing doesn't happen again?'

9 **Investigate the causes of bad behaviour.** Talk – on a one-to-one basis away from the class – to a pupil who has caused problems and try to find out the reasons for misbehaviour. Sometimes, the reasons (once known) will be very understandable and forgivable.

10 **Have ready something interesting to give the class to do.** This can be invaluable when you need time to calm down yourself, or when you need to have those few quiet words outside the door with an individual pupil who has been causing problems. Prepare a verbal quiz or game for the last ten minutes, either as a reward for work well done, or because you have finished a useful activity and need a change.

6

Using blackboards

There's a blackboard or whiteboard in most teaching rooms. We sometimes feel so close to this in our professional lives that the term 'life at the chalk-face' is in common use! How we use it can make a big difference to how much our pupils learn.

1 **How visible are your etchings?** Check that the size of your writing is such that the pupils who are furthest away from the board can read what you have written.

2 **Aim for the top!** Ensure that you make good use of the upper half of the board, and only use the rest of the board if you know that pupils at the back aren't screened from viewing by those closer to the board.

3 **Show your agenda.** Use the board to write questions that you will be discussing, so pupils can continue to see the questions as you develop with them the answers.

4 **If you are left-handed, you may find writing on the blackboard difficult.** This is not your ineptitude, but because you are pushing the chalk. It has taken some teachers years of distress to discover this! Left-handed chalk-users (eg PR) sometimes find that standing a little more to the right than usual, and pulling the chalk that bit more, helps improve the situation.

5 **Be heard as well as seen.** Don't talk to the class while you're writing on the board with your back to them. When possible, arrange the room so that you can maintain eye-contact with most of your pupils even while you're writing on the board.

6 **Be prepared!** Whenever possible, prepare a blackboard in advance for a class, so that pupils can see an outline of the things you're going to talk about in the forthcoming lesson straightaway.

7 **Get your pupils' words on to the blackboard.** Whenever you can, use the blackboard to write up things that pupils tell you in answer to your questions, so that they can see their thinking being valued and acknowledged by you.

8 **Let pupils have a turn with the chalk.** Make the blackboard 'everyone's' territory. Ask pupils to write things on it, for example questions they want to ask, ideas they want to discuss and interesting things they want to talk about.

9 **Use the blackboard as a classroom resource.** Give groups of pupils 'blackboard tasks', for example when starting a new topic, ask groups to compose and write up 'ten questions we want to know about it'.

10 **Be careful with the rubber!** Before you erase comments suggested or written by pupils, give a further acknowledgement of the value of these comments.

7

Organizing practical lessons

Practical lessons can so easily turn into chaos if not well organized, however well planned the content is. Don't try anything new with a class unless you have done it yourself in advance and know it works – and save time in demonstrating by showing 'the one you made earlier'.

1 **Check through the materials you require before the lesson starts.** Ensure they are prepared for use. You can waste many minutes (seems like hours) trying to unscrew a jar whilst the class gets bored and runs riot.

2 **Assemble your materials in labelled boxes or trays.** This is well worth doing when it is a lesson you will repeat, and can save you much time organizing the same materials in future.

3 **Engage the help of the class.** Let pupils help to distribute materials and equipment, and in cleaning up at the end of the session. It will save you time and help pupils learn how to look after resources. Allow plenty of time for clearing up; it may take much longer than you think in the early stages.

4 **Make sure you have enough materials for everyone.** Or at least have enough for pupils to work in pairs. When pupils are not fully involved themselves, they tend to experiment in ways you would not approve!

5 **Give short, clear instructions about the task required.** Ask questions of those pupils who seem not to be concentrating to ensure that they have understood. Their repetition of the requirements of the task will reinforce the instructions to the others.

6 **Make demonstrations snappy.** When you are demonstrating an activity or an experiment it is easy to take so long explaining the 'right' way of doing something that pupils who are itching to try it themselves at first become turned off.

7 **Establish firm rules of behaviour.** Disruption or silliness may prove not only counter-productive to learning, but can turn out to be very dangerous.

8 **Avoid the necessity for pupils to queue for your advice or opinion.** Teach pupils to be self-reliant and resourceful, and to help each other if they can't do something or find something.

9 **Bring the class back together at intervals.** Talk to the whole class during activities. Everyone may be working at a different rate, and some pupils will need this structure to avoid being left behind.

10 **Evaluate the activity.** Make time towards the end of a practical lesson for some kind of evaluation. You may not have had time to get round to every individual, and in this way you can ensure that all pupils receive some feedback.

8

Doing yard/bus/break duties painlessly

'Oh no, not all this as well?' you may have exclaimed! Sadly, being a teacher is not just about teaching. We also need to help keep the school going during the times when we're not teaching. The following suggestions may help you tackle this with equanimity!

1 **Get a whistle!** Don't worry that they are a bit old-fashioned. They can help you gain attention in noisy circumstances – as long as you don't over-use them and you gauge the context of the school appropriately.

2 **Make sure you know the rules.** Know what is allowed and what is not. Try to get a thorough briefing from an experienced colleague who can show you the ropes.

3 **Be seen, and heard!** Should you need to enter the toilets or go behind the bike shed, announce your presence loudly. You are less likely to have unpleasant surprises that way!

4 **Wrap up warm on cold days – and be prepared for rain!** Such duties are made more miserable than ever if you are unsuitably dressed. If you can get a hot drink as well, so much the better.

5 **Try pairing up with a colleague.** If your duties turn out to be a hard chore for you, you can either keep each other company or cover each other for short periods so that you each get some sort of break. A 20-minute yard-duty can feel a lot longer than two 10-minute half-duties. If possible, shadow a colleague on the relevant duty before your actual turn comes up, so that you know what may be expected of you before you tackle it on your own.

6 **Pave the way.** Try to be especially well-prepared in advance if you know you will be teaching immediately after a duty. This can ensure that you are not too flustered at the start of the ensuing lesson. Give the class something to do that really keeps them busy while you get your breath back!

7 **Have contingency plans for what to do if things go wrong.** Check out what the school policy is on minor accidents or incidents. With younger pupils, it may be useful to have readily available supplies of antiseptic wipes and plasters.

8 **Keep your eyes peeled!** It isn't possible to have your eyes everywhere, but you can often prevent trouble by stepping in before it happens. The price of peace is eternal vigilance!

9 **If fights break out, think carefully about your interventions.** You can restrain pupils using 'reasonable force' where the safety of a pupil or a colleague is threatened, but these conditions may not be easy to interpret. Under no circumstances should you ever strike a pupil.

10 **Use such duties as occasions when you can build up good relations with pupils outside the classroom.** Be careful, however, not to put yourself at risk of seeming to have favourites, or of giving excessively exceptional attention to particular individual pupils.

9

Ensuring equality of opportunity within your teaching

The suggestions in this section relate to anti-oppressive practice in all areas, including race, gender, sexuality, age and disability. It is increasingly necessary in our society to tackle inequality head-on, and the sooner the better. The following suggestions should help you treat all pupils equally, and help them to value equality.

1 **Check that you are behaving in the same way towards all pupils.** Check that you are not treating pupils, whatever their background, differently in lessons, when you ask questions or let pupils give comments.

2 **Arrange that the group work is done in mixed-gender groups.** At certain ages pupils' natural tendency is to sit in same-gender groupings, and you may have to intervene in natural seating arrangements. Don't work from gender lists when arranging groups, use a more random characteristic such as birth dates.

3 **Get your tongue round *all* your pupils names!** Make an effort to be able to pronounce the names of pupils with names unfamiliar to you, without any hesitation or insecurity. Allow them to keep telling you whether you've got their names right or not yet.

4 **Avoid discriminatory type-casting.** In designing class exercises, case-studies or scenarios, ensure that you are not type-casting roles according to race, gender, sexuality, age or disability. Also, avoid the tendency to ask only boys to help move furniture, lift boxes, open jars and bottles, or to ask only girls to tidy up or clean benches.

5 **Help colleagues to avoid discrimination.** Be sensitive to instances where colleagues violate equal opportunities principles, and bring such occasions to their notice.

6 **Watch your sense of humour!** It is dangerously easy to attempt to say something amusing, when in fact the fun is at someone's expense. Do not use jokes or anecdotes which could be interpreted as oppressive to any group.

7 **Raise pupils' awareness of equality issues.** Encourage pupils to confront issues of inequality objectively, and help them to work out practical and viable solutions to problems involving equal opportunity.

8 **Be on the lookout for pupils who may be affected by inequality.** Seek feedback from all pupils to probe any feelings they may have regarding being treated unequally in any respect.

9 **Reflect equality in your own work.** Proactively seek to work collaboratively with colleagues of different race, gender, sexuality, age and ability, whenever the opportunity arises.

10 **Don't let pupils get away with bias.** Censure any pupils who display inappropriate bias in things they say or write, and help them towards attitudes which enable them to demonstrate equality values.

Part 2 Planning and Assessment

10

Assessing pupils' work

It often feels that we spend more time marking pupils' work than teaching them. This is probably no bad thing, providing pupils are gaining much from the feedback we give them. The following suggestions may help you enhance this feedback, and at the same time ease your marking load.

1   **Prepare and share your marking schemes.** When designing assessed tasks for pupils, work out in advance the marking scheme you will use to assess their work, and give them clear pointers about what will gain them marks. There is clear evidence that the more pupils know about how assessment works, the better is the standard of work they produce.

2   **Let pupils contribute to the assessment criteria.** From time to time, involve pupils themselves in the task of working out marking schemes for their work, and use their suggestions in your assessment of their work.

3   **Design tasks which are straightforward to assess.** Save yourself time and energy by making it easier to mark pupils' work. For example, it is much quicker to mark their answers to printed short-answer or completion questions, or multiple choice tests, than to work through a pile of essays.

4   **Keep clear records.** Design your own grids so that you can see at a glance the performance of all of the pupils in a class. These can alert you to those pupils falling behind in their work, and can be very useful at parent-teacher interviews.

5   **Make room for your own feedback.** For example, get pupils to pencil-in a fairly substantial margin at one side of the paper, or even to pencil-off a feedback comments box at the foot of each page.

6   **Be aware of pupils' feelings when receiving assessed work back.** Remember that the moment when pupils get back some marked work is a time of heightened emotion for them. This means that they can be particularly sensitive to any comments you have written on their work, especially the first comments they read.

7   **Remember the importance of scores or grades.** When you give pupils a score or a grade, this is the first thing they look for and will dominate their reactions to your comments on their work. If the score is high, they may ignore most of your feedback comments. If the score is low they may be so dispirited that they don't read any feedback comments at all. Decide whether giving a score is important, or whether it may be worth giving only feedback comments at first, and working out the scores later.

8   **Be careful with the crosses.** Remember how demotivating crosses beside mistakes or wrong answers can be. Similarly, crossed-out words (for example where wrongly spelt) can be discouraging. Explore other ways of showing pupils their mistakes, such as using a fluorescent highlighter pen to pick out words and phrases, with margin notes giving explanations.

9   **Look for better things than ticks.** Ticks are good news for pupils, but it's often worth adding some positive feedback comments such as 'good point', 'nicely put', 'well done', which are even more encouraging.

10 **Give pupils the chance to redeem a poor assessment.** For example, use schemes where the best five out of eight assessments make up the coursework grade.

11

Giving pupils face-to-face feedback

Face-to-face feedback to pupils can be very powerful and productive, but it can also be traumatic both for them and for us. The following suggestions may help you to maximize the benefits of such feedback, while minimizing the dangers.

1 **Remember pupils' feelings.** Remember that pupils can feel quite tense when getting face-to-face feedback from a teacher. They may see us both as experts and authority figures. The tension can cause them to receive our feedback in a distorted way, where they take our words beyond the actual messages we wish to convey.

2 **Use the benefits of face-to-face feedback.** Face-to-face feedback can give pupils much more information than written feedback, through facial expression, tone of voice, body language.

3 **Beware of the lost impact.** The main problem with face-to-face feedback is that it is transient. This means that pupils can't reflect objectively on this sort of feedback, as human nature means that they will remember particular parts of the feedback and forget other parts.

4 **Don't forget the dangers of subjective reactions.** Pupils' states of mind can affect their receptiveness to face-to-face feedback. If they happen to be feeling positive and optimistic at the time, they may remember the positive parts of your feedback, while if they are feeling tense or negative at the time, the parts they will remember most will be the critical things you tell them.

5 **Check that your messages are getting across.** An advantage of face-to-face feedback is that you can observe at once the effect that your words are having on pupils. When you can tell that your message is not yet getting across, you can go into more detail.

6 **Decide what to tell individuals, and what to share with groups.** It's worth deciding when best to give face-to-face feedback to individual pupils, and when to give feedback to pupils in groups. Highly specific feedback is best saved for one-to-one interviews, but it can be worth giving general feedback about common mistakes to groups rather than individuals.

7 **Prepare a written summary.** When you have a lot of feedback to give pupils (particularly to a whole class rather than individuals), it is useful to prepare summary notes of the main points you wish to convey. You may even be able to duplicate these notes, and give them out as permanent reminders of your main points.

8 **Always start and end on a high note.** Sometimes, face-to-face feedback will necessarily be hard for your pupils to take. On such occasions, try to make sure that you have some positive things to say about their work, and start and end with such points.

9 **Watch for the effects on pupils.** A strong advantage of face-to-face feedback is that you can judge the effect it is having on pupils, from their facial expressions and body language. If they appear to be particularly sensitive to your comments, you can soften your approach accordingly.

10 **Face-to-face feedback is always two-way.** Exploit the opportunity of using face-to-face feedback occasions to find out more from your pupils about how they feel their learning is going. Asking questions such as 'Why do you think you're finding this difficult?' can be useful.

12

Getting feedback from pupils

Your teaching will be more effective if you are aware of what the pupils' responses and future needs are. It is easy to go through the day without being self-reflective about your work – most of the time you are too busy! But try to make some time to reflect on how your pupils are responding to the work and whether you are having any success.

1   **Look everywhere for feedback.** The expressions on pupils' faces are an immediate source of feedback. The way they respond to your tasks and instructions is feedback.

2   **Ask pupils for general feedback.** Ask open-ended questions. Allow pupils time to work out exactly what the questions mean, and to respond without feeling embarrassed or intimidated.

3   **Help pupils give you specific feedback.** Discuss their work with them on a one-to-one basis with the work in front of you. When they have a problem with part of their work, give them the chance to explain why they think the problem is there.

4   **Collect evidence of pupils' views and opinions.** Occasionally give out evaluation sheets or questionnaires designed to seek their feedback on specific issues.

5   **Don't make a big thing of 'silly' feedback.** There will always be someone who can't resist giving non-serious answers to evaluation questions. Concentrate on the feedback that is useful.

6   **Accept positive feedback.** Resist the urge to shrug off compliments. Give pupils who have positive things to tell you the satisfaction of knowing that their feedback is being received, not stifled.

7 **Accept negative feedback too!** Cultivate the attitude that there is no such thing as criticism, just feedback. Be willing to listen, and to help to draw out any negative feedback from pupils. Better still, thank them for their comments, for example saying 'I'm glad I now know about this; I'll give it further thought, thanks'.

8 **Help pupils to feel that their comments and ideas are valuable.** Ask for positive and constructive criticism on a particular aspect of the course – explain that you might be redesigning it for future classes.

9 **Collect feedback from groups as well as individuals.** You are less likely to get unconsidered feedback from a group than from an individual. Ask pupils to discuss their work in small groups and ask each group to report back to the rest of the class about how they think their work is progressing.

10 **Get further feedback from your colleagues.** When asked, colleagues are often able to give us further feedback about what they've gathered from pupils about our teaching.

13

Using self- and peer-assessment

The main advantages of using self-assessment and peer-assessment are that pupils find out more about how the assessment system works, and become better able to adjust their approaches to gain credit for their learning. The following suggestions may help you take advantage of these benefits.

1   **Help pupils to see the benefits of measuring their own work,** as a means of looking more deeply at what they have done.

2   **Equip pupils with a set of assessment criteria that they understand** and can apply to their work. Where possible, involve pupils in working out for themselves the best way of wording the criteria, to give them a sense of ownership of the assessment agenda.

3   **Never mind the score, feel the learning!** Advise pupils self-assessing their own work that the most important outcome is not the score or mark they award themselves, but the decisions they make as they apply assessment criteria to their work.

4   **Trust pupils' judgement.** Avoid the reaction that pupils engaged in self-assessment will be far too kind to themselves. While *some* pupils may do this, most are rather harder on their own work than we ourselves may have been.

5   **Don't interfere lightly.** Rather than re-mark pupils' self-assessed work and give them 'our' scores as a comparison, it is better to give them feedback on the quality of their own self-assessment, and ask them to adjust their assessments on the basis of this feedback.

6   **Use peer-assessment for increased feedback.** Engaging pupils in peer-assessment (where they mark each others' work) can be even more beneficial than self-assessment at times, because of the thinking that pupils do as they apply assessment criteria to their classmates' work, and then check that the criteria have been applied correctly to their own work.

7   **Select appropriate tasks for peer-assessment.** Choose with care the nature of the tasks where pupils peer-assess each others' work. The most suitable tasks are those where pupils can benefit a lot from the informal feedback they can give each other about the work.

8   **Be available as an expert witness.** When pupils are in the process of peer-assessing, offer to give 'judgements' on particular issues, making sure that all pupils are aware of these finer points regarding the inter- pretation of the assessment criteria.

9   **Allow for renegotiation of peer-assessed scores.** Act as adjudicator when pupils feel that their scores have been rated too low (though don't expect them to complain if they have been rated too high!).

10   **Don't be thought to be abdicating your responsibilities.** Be careful not to impose self-assessment or peer-assessment against pupils' will. They need to be convinced of the benefits for them in terms of deeper learn- ing, otherwise they may feel that you are ducking out of something that they feel is your job.

14

Making sense of GNVQ

Introducing new courses such as GNVQ can seem a nightmare if you have not previously taught in vocational education. A different philosophy prevails – and, as in most teaching, if you can understand the methods of assessment you will soon be able to cope with ways to present the content. In particular, the key to GNVQs lies in pupils accumulating appropriate *evidence* of their achievements as matched against the performance criteria outlined in the specifications.

1 In setting tasks or assignments, **ensure that the performance criteria to be met are clearly identified to the pupils.** Where necessary, translate the 'official' performance criteria into words which pupils can understand easily.

2 **Ensure that the tasks set will generate the evidence** needed if carried out properly. Give a range of examples to pupils, to help them see the sorts of evidence they should aim to accumulate as they work through GNVQ programmes.

3 **Plan to cover Optional Units at the same time as Mandatory Units where this is possible.** In particular, help to reinforce the connections between things pupils do for Optional Units and Mandatory Units.

4 **Help pupils see how a particular task can relate to several parts of their GNVQ programme.** Spend time mapping out where more than one performance criterion, aspect of the range, or Unit can be covered simultaneously.

5 **Encourage pupils to cross-reference their own work on a GNVQ programme,** identifying performance criteria and achievements as they do them rather than retrospectively. Make sure that pupils have their own copies of the GNVQ documentation, and help them make sense of the terminology where necessary!

6 **Record examples of pupils' attainment in Core Skills as they happen,** with a note explaining the skill displayed and the date. This can act as hard evidence of attainment. Encourage pupils to offer spontaneous alternative examples of work they have done which demonstrates their 'Core Skills' achievements.

7 **Set short deadlines for the completion of Units** – it is always easier to progress if you can establish early on what has already been covered, and have plenty of time left for things which are still outstanding.

8 **Encourage peer assessment and group discussion** on attainment of the performance criteria across the range required. Get pupils to help each other in tracking their coverage of the range and performance criteria, and in keeping their logbooks up to date.

9 **Pay particular attention to the nature of 'good' evidence.** When pupils know 'what it looks like to have been shown to have succeeded', they can focus their efforts accordingly.

10 **Avoid feeling alienated by the GNVQ Specifications!** We can all think of other things that we feel should have been included in such specifications, and things that are included that we think are irrelevant. We can indeed adjust our teaching to cover the things we believe should be there, but at the end of the day, we need our pupils to be able to present evidence which matches the Specifications as they are.

15

Planning schemes of work

As you know, thorough planning is essential in the modern classroom if you are to succeed in covering all aspects of the National Curriculum. It will become second nature to you to spend a great deal of time on this aspect of your work. But make sure you leave some room for manoeuvre – teachers perform best when they are really interested in the topic, or when they digress to cover something which is particularly relevant on that day. Give yourself leeway to adapt your schemes of work to react to topical issues and enjoy fitting what the pupils need to know to what you care about!

1 Although an overall plan for the whole school year is necessary, **it is not wise to plan in detail for more than a few weeks ahead.** If you do this the chances are that circumstances may change and your planning may be inappropriate. One of the features of a good scheme of work is adaptability.

2 Before you start to plan, **ask yourself what skills are to be learned and what knowledge is to be gained by the pupils.** It is, after all, their learning outcomes that are the basis of any effective plan.

3 **Ensure that your teaching aims and objectives are clearly stated.** You may find it useful to re-compose these aims and objectives following the phrase: 'what this really means for my pupils is . . .'.

4 **Think in advance of the ability range you expect.** Make sure that your plans allow highly able pupils to flourish, but also accommodate the needs and competences of the less able.

5 **Plan your assessments as early as possible.** Indicate the types of assessment you intend to use. Make sure that the things that are to be assessed link demonstrably to the aims and objectives you intend your pupils to achieve. Bring variety into your assessment processes, so that pupils with different abilities have their own chance to show themselves at their best in one or other form of assessment.

6   **Specify what the expected outcomes will be.** This is best done in terms of the evidence that pupils will be expected to provide to demonstrate their achievement of the objectives. Work out which of the outcomes will be assessable, and how you will approach assessing them.

7   **Include coverage of cross-curricular themes and dimensions where appropriate.** Incorporate issues such as equal opportunities, economics, business awareness and citizenship where appropriate, and highlight the coverage in your planning and schemes of work.

8   **Identify what resources will be needed and when.** This is best done at the planning stage, to allow time to obtain particular resources relating to individual objectives and learning outcomes.

9   **Plan the time-scale for covering the objectives.** It is often best to cover as much as possible during the first half of a teaching year, to allow ample time for revision and consolidation of pupils' achievements well before final assessments are made.

10 **Acknowledge your own professional instincts and experience.** When teaching to 'a formula', it is all too easy to feel devalued and disenfranchised. However, with a bit of planning, it is often possible to mould your own perception of how you would like to teach a subject, and match it into even the most rigid-looking framework.

16

Invigilating internal exams

Sitting written exams is one of the most stressful parts of life for many pupils. Because of the need to prevent cheating and ensure a quiet environment, examination rooms can be very hostile! Invigilating exams can be very tedious, but it is a highly responsible part of your work. If candidates get away with cheating, it will be regarded as your fault. The following suggestions may help you to invigilate fairly and kindly. (Remember that there will be specific regulations for external exams.)

1 **Minimize the possibilities of pupils cheating.** Tell them to leave bags in a pile at the front of the room, and before starting the exam remind them to double check that they have nothing on their person that could be interpreted as a crib. Remind them to check pockets and pencil cases.

2 **Get your timing right.** Ensure that examinations start and finish promptly, and keep pupils informed verbally about the progress of time. Occasional comments such as 'one hour left to go', '30 minutes left', and so on, can help pupils who have lost track of the progress of time.

3 **Try not to intimidate nervous pupils.** Be as unobtrusive as you can, while maintaining your vigilance. You will often see more by positioning yourself behind the candidates, in an aisle.

4 **Keep pupils well supplied with paper.** Walk round occasionally carrying extra paper, and when you can see that a pupil is about to need more, provide some without the need of the pupil asking.

5 **Keep records of the seating arrangement.** If when marking scripts it becomes suspected that some pupils have succeeded in collaborating, the seating records can often disprove or point further towards the suspicion.

6 **Act quickly but quietly if you find pupils cheating.** Write on the front of their scripts an appropriate note (for example: 'Incident at 09.42, involving also Janet Davies'), and make your own notes about exactly what you saw, and what you may suspect.

7   **Have arrangements in place for pupils who need the toilet.** If you're invigilating alone you can't leave the classroom or examination hall personally to escort such pupils there, but you can have a system where there is someone you can call in to see to such events.

8   **With externally-set papers, follow the Examination Board regulations to the letter.** In particular, ensure that candidates' scripts bear their names or candidate numbers as required, and that any loose sheets or graphs are fully identifiable.

9   **Be kind and supportive to pupils suffering from exam stress.** Even a smile from you can help relieve their stress. Sometimes you may need to enable a very tense pupil to be escorted from the room for a breath of fresh air. Highly tense or faint-feeling pupils may feel less stressed if they take their exam right at the back of the room, where they feel fewer eyes are on them.

10   **Be ready to solve problems arising from the question-paper.** With internal papers, if pupils bring to your attention a mistake or omission in a question, alert the whole group to leave this question alone for the time being, and send for the teacher who wrote the question to adjudicate. With external papers, it may be possible to arrange for someone to telephone the Examination Board.

17

Writing reports

This is always a tedious business, coming as it often does at the end of a busy term. You may have hundreds of reports to write of pupils you may see only once a week, and you may be short of time to do it in. However, to each parent theirs is the only one that matters. To do each pupil justice, you need to prepare continuously for report-writing, rather than leave it until the last minute. It's a good idea if you are new to the job to check out the school policy on reports.

1 **Keep careful notes about each pupil's achievements throughout the year.** This will save you time later. File and record all of their marked work so that you can base your report on clear evidence rather than estimation.

2 **When you are inexperienced, write your reports out in rough first,** then transfer them onto the requisite sheets when you are satisfied with them. This will slow you down initially, but will help you to avoid errors and problems, especially when you are writing composite reports with other teachers.

3 **Make sure when you refer to a pupil by name, that you get it right!** If a pupil is generally known by a shortened version of the name, using this can make the report less formal.

4 **Make reports constructive.** Try to use each report as an opportunity to give advice on how the pupil can improve, rather than just a means of passing judgement.

5 **Be sensitive regarding whom the report is going to.** Don't assume that everyone lives in a nuclear family. If parents live apart, it is helpful to let both have copies of the report.

6 **Make sure that what you write is readable and accurate.** If the report is handwritten, make sure that your writing is up to it. If you use a typewriter or word processor, make sure that the print quality is acceptable, not too faint, and contains no typographical errors. Check and double-check your spelling: nothing gives parents a worse impression than a teacher who cannot spell! (One of us always remembers an entry on his own report: 'spelling dissappointing!')

7 **Don't use a statement bank clumsily.** Many teachers have a range of comments and sentence elements that they use over and over again for different reports. This can be usefully formalized into a statement bank on a computer or in the mind, so that elements can be called up and combined in different ways to suit each pupil and each report. If this is sensitively done, it can save you time, but beware of writing reports which look as if they have been assembled by a robot. You will need to customize them for each individual pupil if they are not to be meaningless.

8 **Don't try to do too many reports at a time.** Do them in batches so they don't all end up being made of the sorts of banal clichés or unexceptional comments which our brains come up with when they're tired! Do try not to leave writing reports till the last minute.

9 **Respect pupils' rights to privacy.** Don't leave reports lying around in places where they can be read by all and sundry.

10 **Try to avoid surprises.** It may be helpful to let pupils know what you have written about them before their reports go home, especially if the news is bad. Security of transmission of the report to parents or guardians will need to be assured.

18

Preparing for an inspection

The thought of an imminent inspection can be intimidating and stressful to the classroom teacher and often the feeling within the school as the date nears can approach panic. However an inspection can be a valuable experience in helping you to set priorities and identify your own areas of concern. If you are well prepared and have a clear idea of your objectives as a teacher there should be no worries! These suggestions, however, cannot possibly cover everything the OFSTED handbook includes – we simply give a few hints on how to approach the ordeal!

1 As a member of a department, **ensure that all the necessary policies and documentation are in place** as part of the pre-Inspection evidence. If you are aware of areas of concern make sure that you have identified them as a department and have some strategy in place to begin to tackle them.

2 Ensure that any **departmental policies are in line with whole-school policies,** for example on assessment, equal opportunities, or discipline.

3 **Ensure that all the written policies are actually being implemented** and that all colleagues are aware of their practical application. Try to gather evidence of the implementation of each policy, so that you can add detail to the rhetoric when necessary.

4 **Make sure that you have a clear idea of what you are doing and why** – both on a long-term and a short-term basis! Make links between the way you go about your day-to-day work with pupils, and the whole-school policies and aims.

5 **Have clear written schemes of work and individual lesson plans** which show how what you are teaching fits into the National Curriculum programmes of study or external examination syllabuses.

6 **Make it clear how what you do can be measured.** Ensure that what you are teaching – and what pupils are learning – can be assessed, and make it clear how and when this will happen.

7 **Be ready to show how you approach mixed-ability groups.** Ensure that your lessons are differentiated to meet the needs of pupils of all abilities.

8 **Be prepared to demonstrate variety.** Get in the habit of teaching structured lessons which allow for a range of activities and learning experiences.

9 **Be ready to show that you are well prepared and resourced.** Ensure that adequate resources are available and accessible by pupils – label your drawers, stores, bookshelves, and so on. Demonstrate that pupils have access to facilities for independent learning.

10 **Be prepared to demonstrate the breadth as well as the depth!** Try to identify where you can cover cross-curricular themes and dimensions within your subject teaching and build this into your planning.

Part 3 Using Teaching and Learning Resources Well

19

Preparing interesting handout materials

With the availability of photocopiers and offset litho printing, it is increasingly preferable to use handout materials rather than relying on class-issued textbooks. The following suggestions may help you create handouts which are used actively by pupils, rather than simply filed away with their notes. Of course, you may need to collect in and reuse handouts where resources are limited. In such cases it may pay you to laminate the handouts.

1 **Try to make handouts look attractive and interesting.** Where possible, include pictures and illustrations, so that the materials are attractive for pupils to use. A box or edging makes all the difference.

2 **Make it clear what each handout is about.** Use clear headings so that pupils can quickly identify each handout. It can be worth having a numbered set of handouts, and a separate index page so that pupils can file them in the correct order when the set is complete.

3 **Present the objectives.** Start each handout with a clear statement of what the handout is for in terms of the things pupils will be able to do once they have worked through it. Such statements can convey the intended objectives of the handout, or the expected learning outcomes.

4 **Use handouts in an interactive way.** Include tasks and activities for pupils to do as they work through the handouts. These can include things to be done in class, and also things to be done as homework tasks.

5 **Provide white space for pupils to write on.** Include boxes for pupils to write in their answers to questions in the handouts. When pupils have their own writing on handouts, it adds to their sense of ownership of them.

6 **Organise your collection of handouts.** Keep a separate file containing the master copy of each handout, and separate files or boxes containing copies of each handout for issue to pupils.

7 **Share your resources.** Make an additional set of copies of your handouts available to other colleagues, in a central location such as a staffroom filing cabinet. Encourage colleagues to share their own handouts in a similar way.

8 **Make handouts which help pupils who are absent.** Create special handouts covering the most important topics in your subject, suitable for pupils who miss important lessons. These handouts may also be useful as revision aids for all pupils nearer their exams.

9 **Build assessment into handouts.** Include self-tests towards the end of each handout, so that pupils can check for themselves how much they already understand, and how much further work they may need to do on the materials.

10 **Make it easy to update handouts.** If possible, have your handout materials stored on computer-disk or desktop publishing systems, so that you can continuously make minor adjustments and improvements to the handouts, without having to recompose them from scratch.

20

Preparing learning packages

Open or flexible learning packages have many advantages, including enabling pupils to work though selected parts of the curriculum at their own pace, in their own way, and where and when they want to work on them. The following suggestions may help you to design packages of your own, or make good use of existing ones with your pupils.

1 **Work out what pupils can do by themselves.** Identify the parts of the curriculum which may lend themselves best to pupils using learning packages rather than taught lessons.

2 **Make the objectives clear.** Work out clear statements of the intended learning outcomes of learning packages that you design or use. Make sure that pupils understand exactly what they are aiming to learn to do as a result of working through each learning package.

3 **Design packages around things for pupils to do – not just to read.** Ensure that learning packages contain plenty of activity for pupils. Make sure that the tasks and activities in the packages are clearly phrased, and that pupils understand exactly what they are supposed to do.

4 **Package your feedback as well as the activity.** Make sure that each time pupils have a go at a task or activity, there is readily available feedback, so that they can self-assess their work. The feedback may be provided in print in the packages (out of sight of the task questions), or could be delivered personally by yourself.

5 **'Why did I get this wrong?'** Remember that pupils need to know not only whether they approached a task correctly – if they got it wrong, they need guidance as to what went wrong. Check that the feedback they receive covers this.

6 **Learning packages aren't textbooks.** Make it clear to pupils how learning packages are unlike textbooks. Learning packages are things for them to do, not just to read. They will learn much more from having a go at the tasks and activities, than just from reading the information in the packages.

7 **Test out the bits of your package.** Experiment with components of learning packages in class, where you can monitor how pupils handle them. Take particular note of pupils' problems, and add extra guidance to the packages on this basis.

8 **Measure what is happening.** Include or add an end-test of one kind or another, which pupils will hand in for marking when they finish working through a package. Use this not only to check their achievements, but to identify any trouble-spots in the learning package.

9 **Give pupils guidance.** When using an existing learning package, it can be well worth adding a brief set of guidance notes on 'how to approach using this package', highlighting the most important parts of the package, and the best ways of tackling it.

10 **Show pupils where the package fits into their overall course.** Remember to make sure pupils know how much the things they learn when using learning packages count for in their overall course.

21

Using videos in the classroom

With television sets in continuous use in many homes, there is the temptation to regard television images as 'wallpaper' rather than sources of learning-experience. When using television or video in lessons, the following suggestions may help you to ensure that effective learning results.

1 **Know how the machine works!** Make sure you are familiar with the operation of the video machine, and that it is properly connected up. Since most pupils will be able to operate such machines, it is embarrassing when we can't!

2 **Be ready to start.** If using a videotape, get the tape to the position you want to start from! (It seems to take ages to find the right starting point when all eyes are watching us trying to do so!).

3 **Make sure everyone can see properly.** Rearrange the furniture if necessary, so that pupils have as clear a view of the screen as possible. It is often best to dispense with desks, and just use chairs – or indeed the floor.

4 **Know why you're using a video.** Have a clear purpose for using each episode of television or video. Decide what you intend your pupils to get out of it, and let them know this.

5 **Help pupils know why they're watching.** Work out with your pupils an agenda of questions to which they wish to find out the answers, before watching a programme. Their concentration will be increased when they are looking for specific things from the programme.

6 **Decide how much to show.** Remember that concentration spans are short – particularly when using a medium that is associated with relaxation or 'background'. A few selected 'clips' may be just as useful as a full 30-minute programme.

7 **Use video to advantage.** Analyse the particular benefits of using television images, for example the messages conveyed by facial expression and tone of voice, body language and so on. Alert pupils to things they can deduce as they observe the programme.

8 **Work out how to capture the main learning points.** Since we are conditioned to forget quickly most of what we see on television screens, work out ways of capturing the most important points from the programme. This may best be done by pausing now and then and asking pupils questions, or discussing the implications of what they have just seen.

9 **Get the main points down on paper.** Where important learning outcomes are to be derived from a programme, work out ways that the products of the viewing can be transferred to paper. For example, put together a handout for learners to complete after watching the programme, so that they record their conclusions in a way that they can review at any time later.

10 **What, another repeat?** When a programme covers something really important, remember the benefits of seeing it more than once. We all see things we had not noticed before when we view a programme for the second time.

22

Getting the most from the library

School libraries and learning resources rooms may contain large amounts of useful information; the problem is helping pupils to make the most of them. Don't assume that pupils know how to use libraries or have often visited them. The following suggestions may help them make good use of such resources.

1 **Spell out the benefits to pupils.** Explain to pupils how useful it is to become good at tracking down relevant information in libraries (public libraries as well as at school). Explain how much time it can save them, when finding information to use in writing essays or reports.

2 **Give pupils useful practice.** Set tasks or projects which require pupils to track down particular reference materials you know are in the library or resource centre. Plan the tasks so that pupils become familiar with the ways the materials are catalogued or indexed.

3 **Help pupils develop their searching skills.** Help pupils to develop their skills at focusing on the most relevant materials. Give them clear guidelines to help them know exactly what they are looking for in the materials they consult.

4 **Help pupils to get their references right.** Train pupils in the correct way to refer to the sources of information they quote. Make sure that in your own lessons and handouts you refer to materials precisely (for example: Saunders, D (ed) (1994) *The Complete Student Handbook* Blackwell, Oxford).

5 **Encourage groups of pupils to use the library.** Give pupils group exercises to do, using materials in the library, helping them to pick up from each other valuable tracking and retrieval skills.

6 **Value the expertise of library staff where you have them.** Remind pupils how useful librarians' help can be. Many public or college libraries have subject librarians, who have a good understanding of their own subjects as well as excellent knowledge of the available books in the field.

7 **Encourage pupils to use their eyes in a library!** For example, when there are several copies of a book, or when particular books are well-thumbed, it is probable that these are more useful sources of information than an 'unused-looking' book.

8 **Remind pupils that modern libraries don't just contain books.** They also contain audio-visual materials, CD-ROM databases, and computer-assisted learning packages.

9 **Encourage pupils to make useful notes** when using materials in a library or resource centre. Remind them to make careful notes of which sources they extract information from, so they can locate particular sources again quickly when they need to.

10 **Alert pupils to the usefulness of contents pages and indexes** when working out whether a particular book is relevant to what they want to find out. This can be far quicker than simply scanning through the book itself.

23

Organizing resources

If your room is well organized and ordered, pupils are more likely to respond by tidying up themselves. Giving pupils access to resources also helps them begin to take responsibility for their own learning and progress. Both you and your pupils will have a clearer idea of what is available by keeping stock labelled and sorted.

1 **Arrange well-used resources in easily accessible and labelled storage** so that pupils can help themselves, saving your time for more important tasks.

2 Keep small items such as pencils, rulers, and so on in **multiples of ten** so that you can easily check on numbers returned. Give responsibility for looking after certain items to a monitor who will give out and collect in books and other items – this saves traffic jams and needless wandering about.

3 **Ensure that there are plentiful supplies of scrap paper,** available for rough work and drafting. Cultivate local supplies of one-sided scrap paper, such as reprographics departments at local colleges or firms.

4 **Keep valuable or destructible resources locked away.** However, don't make it appear that these resources are unavailable to pupils; instead help them to see for themselves that they need to handle these resources with care.

5 **Use boxes, jars and trays to keep small items together.** A clear system of labels can turn a collection of boxes, jars and trays into an accessible resource collection.

6 **Emphasise the need to respect tools, materials and equipment** and the need to use them carefully and safely. It is easy for pupils to abuse resources simply because they do not feel any ownership or realize the value of such resources, or the difficulty in replacing certain items.

7 **Assemble collections of stimulus or source material in labelled boxes** so that pupils can track them down easily and use them independently.

8 **Collect together worksheets and other task-briefings** and keep in accessible storage for pupils who happen to finish work early, or to give them out as 'extension tasks' for more able pupils who may benefit from additional challenges.

9 **Try to make regular times when you sort out your materials and resources.** Weekly is ideal, but half-termly will do. The longer you leave it, the longer it will take you to sort them out ultimately.

10 **Require pupils to take responsibility for the resources they use.** Don't let them get away with sloppy return of materials or incorrect placing of resources. Getting them to take this responsibility necessarily means that you have to ensure that they are allowed sufficient time at the end of class to put things away properly before they rush off to their next session.

24

Making do with limited resources

Unfortunately this is an ever-more-important aspect of the job in these times of Formula Funding and restricted budgets. Teachers have become adept at managing with very little in many areas of the curriculum. So it pays to be aware right from the start that resources are not infinite. When it's gone, it's gone!

1 **Keep a strict eye on stock;** always count in and out small items which are easily taken away (often without thinking). Get one of the more conscientious pupils to take responsibility for certain resources.

2 **Save expensive consumable items for special lessons or the culmination of a project.** Explain to pupils that such items are difficult or impossible to replace, and solicit their help in conserving and protecting them.

3 **Use scrap or recycled materials** – encourage the imaginative and creative use of such resources. Link this to lessons to be learned about environmental issues and conservation.

4 **Prepare your own worksheets and handouts.** This can be much less expensive than giving out published materials.

5 **Help pupils to value resources.** Make sure that pupils are taught the correct way to use materials and equipment and that they understand their cost.

6 **Invite pupils to contribute resources.** Rather than asking for donations, you can ask the class to bring along for the day specified things that may help in the particular lessons to be conducted. Make a 'shopping-list' of resources which would be useful, and ask pupils to put their names besides any items they could bring along. (Make sure, however, that disadvantaged pupils are able to contribute something useful, and don't feel excluded.)

7   **Beg and borrow!** Much as it goes against the grain for professional people who believe that their profession should be adequately resourced, when times are hard, any solution is better than none! When you know exactly what you need, it's well worth asking local businesses or organizations if they can help provide some things on your 'wanted' list.

8   **Use outside sources.** For example, the British Association for the Advancement of Science provides a service of free talks to pupils by practising scientists, who will often bring along a range of expensive equipment to use in demonstrations.

9   **Maintain good contacts with local colleges.** It is often possible to arrange for a school party to visit a college at no charge, for a day which includes opportunities for pupils to use equipment that would not be available at school.

10   **Find out what is available from large companies.** Several large organizations provide a range of education booklets and videos as part of their promotion policies. These materials are usually available on request, at no charge, and can provide the basis of useful class activities.

25

Making your classroom into an attractive learning environment

Secondary schools can often seem alien, impersonal environments where only serious business goes on. Take some tips from primary teachers and put some effort into making your room your own space – after all, you will be spending a good chunk of your life there!

1 **Choose strong, bright and warm colours** if you are given any chance to have your say about the decor. Pupils appreciate such colours much more than the neutrals, and they really do notice! If the room is in need of decoration and funds are not available, use posters, coloured paper and remnants of fabrics to cover the messy bits. The use of different textures and materials can make a cold room much more welcoming.

2 **Display pupils' work to improve the surroundings.** Displays can be attractive, interesting and visually stimulating, and are good educational practice.

3 **Encourage pupils to bring in interesting pictures** to add to displays. They will feel a sense of ownership, and in this way will feel it is also their responsibility to look after their environment.

4 **Use plants to make the room look more attractive and personal.** If you have tutor groups in your room, involve them in taking responsibility for the care and watering of the plants.

5 **'Books do furnish a room'** – as well as being useful to read! They can make a classroom look more interesting. Use colourful designs on book jackets as part of your display – make the layout of the bookshelves accessible and welcoming by providing headings and illustrations.

6 **Carpets are (nearly) magic!** It is increasingly common now for class-rooms to be carpeted, as this is often cheaper than using vinyl; take the option of carpets whenever you have the choice. It not only makes a classroom feel warmer and more pleasant, but it cuts down considerably on noise.

7 **Assemble interesting objects** as well as pictures in your room. You might choose these to relate to what you are teaching, or just because you like them. Unusual items can stimulate creative work in many areas.

8 **Do your own minor maintenance.** For example, if the door is squeaky, oil it. If the door shuts noisily, you may consider sticking the odd strip of draughtproofing strip strategically, to muffle the sound of the door closing.

9 **Rearrange the furniture.** With pupils' help, you can make major transformations in the layout of a classroom quite quickly. They too will usually enjoy the change. It can also be a useful move when you feel that the class geography needs to be adjusted to disperse cliques.

10 **Keep an eye open regarding your access.** Ideally, you need to be able to go right up to any pupils as they are working, to give them individual advice or feedback. Pupils who feel they are safely isolated from you may not do much work!

26

Making effective displays

Classrooms can be made visually interesting with displays of pupils' work and other materials that can stimulate and inform. Don't worry if you feel you have little artistic skill – if you follow a few guidelines you can make anything look attractive.

1   **Pupils' own work will usually be the focal point of a display.** Choose examples from across the ability range – one of the reasons for display-ing work is to show that it is valued. If they have produced good work which is not well presented you can often get them to re-present it more clearly for a special display. Make sure you include pupils' names on their work.

2   **Include photographs, newspaper cuttings, artefacts, fabric, found objects** – anything to add colour, texture and interest. Pictures and other relevant information can make the display informative as well as visually stimulating. Examples of the work of others – writers, poets, scientists, illustrators and artists will also act as stimulus.

3   **Use the display to inform others of the work of your class** – add a few sentences of explanation about your aims and methods in producing the work.

4   **Involve your class in displaying their own work** – they will enjoy this and feel more ownership of the room. But don't forget to teach them what to do! Often they will come up with original and exciting ways of doing it which should be encouraged and facilitated. Get them to word-process some of their work for display, and involve them in pro-ducing headings and illustrations.

5   **Strong, clear lettering is essential** – if you find lettering difficult (who doesn't!) try using a stencil or use computer-generated type. If you use a computer, beware of using too many different founts in one display – two is generally plenty, and vary the effect by changing the size and style. Sometimes handwritten capitals (not bubble writing!) or italics can liven up a dull display. Use simple headings in bold lettering – underlining can look tacky.

6 **The choice of background is important** – if in doubt choose a strong dark colour (you can't go wrong with black sugar paper). If you want a coloured background, pick out and use a predominant colour in the work. Mount light pieces of work on a dark ground and vice versa. If your paper is white and the background is light or medium in tone, it may help to draw a thick black line around the edge of the paper with a marker – this makes the work stand out and is cheaper and less time-consuming than double mounting.

7 If you are double mounting the work, **use a fairly thin border in a contrasting tone.** The size of the borders should be equal on the top and sides but slightly wider at the bottom – this avoids the illusion of the picture appearing to slide off the mount.

8 **It is best to have plenty of visual information on the display** – avoid vast areas of background scattered with small pieces of work. Line up the edges of the work to give an ordered look, or display work diagonally and sometimes overlap to give a more lively effect. Use different shapes – circles, ovals – to mount work on and vary the size of the work displayed.

9 **Change displays regularly.** They can rapidly become part of the scenery. Keep up running repairs to edges and eradicate graffiti – nothing looks worse than a scruffy display.

10 **Consider the use of borders to enhance the display** – choose an appropriate motif and repeat by stencilling or photocopying.

27

Taking pupils on a trip

School trips can be great fun and highly memorable, but they are a terrific responsibility and need meticulous planning. Make sure you are aware of the school or LEA guidelines for taking pupils out of school, and always follow these guidelines to the letter!

1 **Make sure that the parental permission forms go out well in advance.** File all their responses carefully.

2 **Give pupils (and parents) a detailed printed briefing for the trip.** Include full information about the itinerary, with times and places in case anyone should get separated from the group, and a telephone contact number for emergencies.

3 **Plan the visit thoroughly, with sufficient structured activities to keep the pupils occupied productively.** Boredom breeds disruptive behaviour. Use checklists, questionnaires and task sheets (not just written tasks) to help focus pupils' activities.

4 **Make sure you don't lose pupils!** Count them in and out at all times, and delegate individual colleagues and any parent helpers to be responsible for small groups. Never let pupils wander off unsupervised.

5 **Ensure that pupils know the standards of behaviour expected of them before they set off.**

6 **Have with you an emergency kit.** Include first aid equipment, disposable wipes, tissues, sick bucket or bags and so on, as well as spare pens, paper and anything else you think appropriate.

7 **Let pupils know what they are expected to bring with them.** This includes the sort of clothing that will be suitable; any equipment they may need. Also set clear guidelines about what refreshments may be brought, and how much spending money is permitted.

8   **Be where you can see pupils.** When travelling on coaches, you will have better oversight of what pupils are up to if you travel towards the back of the coach, rather than up-front with the driver.

9   **Make productive use of travelling time.** Give pupils observation or discussion tasks, especially on the outward journey when excitement levels may be high.

10 **Follow-up the trip.** Use activities back in the classroom that make best use of the on-site learning pupils may have done. Use assignments in the classroom which allow pupils to draw together what they have learned in the field. Display photos, maps, and pupils' work when appropriate to keep up the momentum well after the trip is over.

28

Visiting museums and art galleries

Visits to galleries and museums can be a most effective learning experience for pupils but they only work really well when adequately prepared. The visit should be the focal point of a topic of work, rather than an additional extra, because so much can result from the opportunity to see at first hand examples of what pupils are studying. The additional stimulus of new surroundings and being out of school can have tremendous benefits.

1 **Visit the museum or gallery beforehand** and decide what you want the pupils to get out of the visit. Any such visit will usually cover many aspects of the curriculum and might be developed into a fully cross-curricular project. Set a few clear objectives for the visit which are integrated into the course of study being followed in school. If appropriate, prepare worksheets, quiz sheets or handouts using what you have learned from the preliminary visit.

2 **Book your party into the museum well in advance** and talk to the Education Officer there about what facilities are on offer. Discuss the best time to visit, and how you will take advantage of any specialist help which may be available.

3 Before your visit, **prepare the pupils well for what they will see and be doing.** If possible show some slides or pictures of exhibits – stimulate their interest beforehand. Sometimes the way a museum or gallery presents itself can seem intimidating or boring to young visitors and they need to understand the reasons for and relevance of their visit.

4 **Plan the work you will do so that it can be developed further back at school.** Visits often take the form of research, stimulus or fact-finding, and more detailed finished work can be produced later.

5 **Allow enough time in the museum or gallery for some practical work** – investigation, recording, drawing. If left to their own devices, pupils may go through the museum very quickly with an unfocused eye. On the other hand sometimes an over-reliance on worksheets or quizzes can mean that they look only for the right answers and ignore any possibilities for individual exploration. Many museums have an Education Room where pupils can have a packed lunch or break, or do follow-up work, or listen to a talk.

6 When there is a lot to see, **split your class into small groups,** to research certain aspects in detail and report back in school.

7 Get the pupils to look critically at **how the work or exhibits are displayed** as well as what is on display. Is there enough explanation offered to the public? Are the displays clearly ordered and attractively presented? You could get pupils subsequently to produce their own mini-gallery or museum in school for other pupils to visit.

8 If possible arrange for an expert or member of the museum staff to give **a short talk about the exhibits.** A new speaker, or acknowledged expert in a subject, will often have more impact than their familiar class teacher.

9 If you can, **arrange for the pupils to be allowed to handle or more closely examine some of the less valuable exhibits.** This can help to make pupils feel 'more special' than casual visitors to the gallery or museum. They could sketch or make notes of these exhibits in closer detail.

10 When the follow-up work is completed back at school, **involve the pupils in displaying what they have done,** bearing in mind the type of display techniques they saw in the museum and how the objects were presented.

Part 4 Supporting Pupils' Learning

29

Helping pupils who don't read well

Not being able to read as well as those around one can seem to pupils like a major catastrophe – particularly in an education system that bases much of its assessment on pupils' skills in reading and writing. The following tips may help redress the balance a little.

1 **Say things as well as writing them.** When setting tasks, provide your briefing orally as well as in writing or print. Make it clear you don't mind repeating the task briefing again for anyone who wishes to *hear* it once more.

2 **Find out who needs help.** Try to identify pupils who have genuine problems with reading, and ensure that they get specialist help from those trained to diagnose and assist pupils with reading problems.

3 **Mind your language!** Use short sentences whenever possible in written tasks and instructions. Reading difficulties are often simply problems in the interpretation of long complex instructions. Consider how the subject-specific vocabulary you use may cause problems to those not familiar with it.

4 **Put reading into perspective.** Remind all pupils that skills in the use of words, and the interpretation of words, are only a small part of what it is to be a successful human being. Remind them that caring, compassion, humour and patience are in fact much more important qualities than the mere ability to use and interpret printed or written words.

5 **Make assessment less dependent on reading skills.** Vary the forms and processes of assessment you employ, so that success does not depend inordinately on pupils' ability to read and interpret written or printed questions. Use spoken questions and instructions as well.

6   **Use some tasks where reading is not too important.** Incorporate tasks and exercises which do not depend on reading skills. Where appropriate, single out pupils for praise, when you know of their problems with tasks which would have involved reading skills.

7   **Help pupils preserve their self-esteem.** Don't allow pupils with reading difficulties to think that they are 'mentally subnormal' or 'strange'. Keep in mind that it is probably just one small area of intelligence that they have problems with, and that they may be highly gifted in other areas.

8   **Help with spelling as well.** Pupils with reading problems often have difficulty with spelling. Identify new vocabulary and help pupils learn to spell new words. 'LCWC' (Look, Cover, Write and Check) is a useful technique for self-help. Spelling ability is not magic: it is essentially a visual skill.

9   **Help pupils gain confidence and motivation.** Spend additional time with pupils who seem to have difficulties interpreting written or printed words. It can sometimes be the case that they just need reassurance and confidence-building.

10   **Never stop explaining.** Use 'WIRMI' – 'What it really means is . . .' as a way of helping pupils put into their own words the meanings of longer sentences or instructions, and encourage pupils to compare interpretations with each other.

30

Helping pupils who don't do maths well

Many people (not least we teachers!) remember their time learning maths at school with little affection. Indeed, this can lead to feelings of mental block against anything numerical or algebraic. Probably, maths is the hardest subject of all to teach really well. The following suggestions focus on how maths is learned best. Try to make maths fun and accessible sometimes. With some imagination (and useful source books) everyday problems – Saturday wages, League Tables, timetables and darts scores – can provide useful practice.

1 **Accept that numbers *are* a foreign language!** They can't be read in the same way as sentences, or heard in long sequences. When pupils have difficulties, try to find out if they understand the stages leading up to the points where their problems are. Maths is about building bricks and if a key brick is missing, the whole process is blocked.

2 **Celebrate mistakes!** Remind pupils that getting something wrong is as useful as getting it right, if the cause of the mistake can be tracked down and isolated. Give praise for each and every stage that is understood and done correctly.

3 **Help pupils detect mistakes for themselves.** From time to time, use a 'spot my mistakes' exercise on the blackboard (or in handout materials). Plan to show pupils the most likely sorts of mistakes they may make, giving them the opportunity to identify the mistakes without the embarrassment of having made them themselves. Develop pupils' feel for the right sort of answer (estimates) so that they become better at recognizing answers which are silly.

4 **Remind pupils of the importance of practice.** Maths is learned by doing maths – not watching someone else do it. Include plenty of practice to help pupils consolidate things they have just learned.

5   **Never mind the speed, is the answer right?** Be careful not to place too much value on speed. Pupils who can do something successfully but slowly are in a position to speed up in due course, but may become entirely demotivated if they feel under immediate pressure to get things right quickly.

6   **Give pupils the chance to learn by explaining.** Let pupils who have got something right explain to others exactly how they did it. They can remember how they learned it themselves, and can often communicate this better than someone who has known it for a long time.

7   **Let pupils see how others tried it.** It is useful to get pupils to mark each other's work in informal tests and exercises. This can alert them to the sorts of mistakes to avoid, as well as to the correct way to approach problems or tasks.

8   **Arrange competition between groups rather than between individuals.** Try getting pupils to work in threes, in a problem-solving game, where each trio is given a different problem (of a similar standard), and the trios compete as to which can solve the most problems in half an hour. There is often no 'right' means to getting the correct answer. Different pupils will understand and use different methods. Try to encourage this in your explanations and praise.

9   **Have practice material at hand.** Have available a bank of handout sheets of problems to practise with, and encourage pupils who need such practice to do them. Give different pupils different sheets, to avoid the wrong sort of collaboration.

10   **Work out your priorities.** For the majority of the class, it is probably more important to cover the basics soundly, rather than to digress into advanced maths. That said, have some difficult problems available to give to those pupils who will respond positively to the challenge.

31

Helping pupils to learn together

Pupils learn a great deal from each other. Often they can understand something more easily when someone who has only just understood it is explaining it to them. Most pupils enjoy working in groups for at least some of the time. The following suggestions may help you get the most from group work.

1 **Be up front with pupils about your reasons for using group activities:** talk to them about the benefits of cooperative learning.

2 **Plan for collaboration rather than competition.** Devise group activities in which tasks can be shared out between group members and expertise can be shared.

3 **Help pupils help each other to learn.** Encourage pupils to quiz each other, giving them practice both in working out sensible questions to ask, and in answering questions informally.

4 **Involve pupils in each other's assessment.** At its simplest level, this could mean checking each other's answers against a model answer given by you. More sophisticated forms of peer assessment can be encouraged subsequently, with pupils giving each other feedback against given or negotiated criteria as their evaluative skills develop.

5 **Give pupils opportunities to teach one another:** teaching someone else something is an excellent way for them to consolidate their own learning (as we teachers know!).

6 **Use different kinds of groups.** When putting pupils into groups for collaborative activity, think about group formation. On different occasions you might like to put them into friendship groups, ability-based groups or learning teams, where you try to balance the range of skills and abilities in each group.

7   **Remain aware of feelings.** Be sensitive about coping with interpersonal problems within groups. There is no point forcing pupils to work together if they can not stand each other. It may be necessary to have contingency plans to change group formations if problems occur.

8   **Avoid passengers.** Monitor group activity to ensure that groups do not carry passengers, prepared to piggy-back on the efforts of others.

9   **Distribute any burdens.** Change the composition of working groups at intervals so that any unpopular or difficult pupils are not always working in the same groups.

10 **Let groups share their products.** Let groups have opportunities to benefit from the learning of other groups through the use of display materials, presentations and so on.

32

Helping pupils revise effectively

Exams measure the quality of pupils' revision more than how long they spent revising. The following suggestions may help your pupils adopt effective and productive approaches to revision.

1 **Prepare revision aids.** All the way through a course, prepare summaries of main points (or get pupils themselves to do this), explaining that these will be useful for later revision, and that it is never too early to start learning from them.

2 **Help pupils know the agenda.** Prepare lists of short questions covering everything important about individual topics and give these to pupils, inviting them to become well-practised at answering the questions.

3 **Get pupils practising.** Use class games where pupils in groups quiz each other using lists of short questions, and keep scores. Suggest ground-rules, such as that if the person who is asked a question cannot answer it, the one who asked it can gain the score for that question by answering it instead.

4 **Show the standards and structures.** Where pupils are heading towards exams, give out copies of old exam papers early in the course, so that they can see the structure of the exams, and the depth of typical questions.

5 **Let pupils in on how the typical examiner's mind may work.** From time to time, set a class exercise around an old exam question, then get pupils to mark each others' answers using the sort of assessment criteria which would have been used in the real exam.

6 **Help pupils to adopt active strategies.** Remind pupils that simply reading something over and over again is a very slow and passive way of trying to learn it. Revision is only active when pupils are applying what they know, and using it to answer questions either in writing or orally.

7   **Help pupils to see how they learn best.** Ask pupils how they learned things (anything at all) that they are already good at. Then remind them that the same processes (learning by practising, and learning from mistakes) can be deliberately applied to things they need to learn for exams.

8   **Encourage pupils to make and use summaries.** Help pupils to make their own concise summaries of the things they need to know. Help them to decide what is important, and what is just background detail.

9   **Help pupils to plan their revision tactics.** Suggest that it is better to do revision in frequent, short spells rather than long, continuous ones. Help pupils to make revision timetables when they are entered for public examinations or end-of-year exams. Remind pupils that everyone's concentration span is quite short, and it is how often they revise something that counts, rather than how long they spend on it in total.

10   **Variety is the spice of revision!** Encourage pupils not to spend too long trying to learn one topic, but to switch topics about every half-hour or so. A change is as good as a rest as far as our brains are concerned – and much more productive than letting boredom set in.

33

Helping pupils to pass exams

Success in exams is as much dependent upon sensible exam techniques as upon subject knowledge. It is sometimes difficult to give pupils sound advice when the system keeps changing, but the following suggestions are intended to help you assist your pupils in developing their exam techniques.

1 **Familiarity breeds confidence.** Especially when heading towards public exams, help pupils to become familiar with the layout and structure of real exam papers, by giving them class and homework opportunities to practise on questions from old papers.

2 **What is the nature of the game?** Remind pupils that exams essentially measure their skills at answering exam questions in writing, and that anyone can improve these skills simply by practising writing such answers.

3 **Stress the importance of good time-management during exams.** Remind pupils that if they spend too long writing too much for question 1, and have no time left for the last two questions, they will have lost far more marks than if they'd done a short answer for question 1 and answered all the other questions.

4 **Help pupils to *analyse* old exam questions**. Ask them to work out what the questions really mean. Help them identify the key words in questions, including 'why?', 'what?', 'how?', 'when?', 'compare', 'explain', 'describe', 'discuss'.

5 **Stress the importance of wise decisions.** When pupils have a choice of questions to make, remind them how important it is to make wise choices concerning which questions they will attempt. The only way of doing this is to read each question slowly, carefully, and more than once.

6 **'Keep checking the questions'.** Suggest to pupils that they should reread the question they're answering several times while writing their answers. This reminds them exactly what the question is asking, and helps them to avoid going off at tangents.

7 **'Show what you're trying to do'.** Emphasize that in numerical or problem-type questions it is important for examiners to be able to see exactly what pupils are trying to do in their answers. If examiners can see the point at which a mistake occurs, they can award marks for the other parts which are correct. If they can't see what went wrong, they can't give any marks at all.

8 **'Don't get stuck and have a mental blank!'** When pupils get stuck on a question because they have forgotten something, encourage them to move on to another question they can answer well, rather than becoming panic-stricken or tense. What matters most is scoring points across the whole paper, rather than getting a particular question entirely right.

9 **Remind pupils that examiners are human** – just like teachers – and they like giving marks for correct answers. Examiners are not simply searching for mistakes. Examiners respond best to clear, well-set-out answers, well-reasoned arguments, and definite conclusions.

10 **'Save time for checking'.** Explain to pupils how useful it is to save several minutes towards the end of each exam, to reread everything they have written, correcting obvious mistakes, and adding important points that may have come to mind since writing the answers.

34

Helping pupils to be creative

It is all too easy when teaching to a syllabus or programme of study to forget that the development of creative or imaginative qualities can be enhanced by your own behaviour in the classroom. You may have a firm idea in your own mind of what you want to teach and may fall into the trap of leaving no leeway for new or unconventional thoughts. Sometimes when work is technically poor or badly presented we may miss its originality or unusual characteristics.

1   In setting a task or project **use a broad task-briefing or a 'neutral stimulus'** so that pupils have plenty of scope for approaching the task in their own ways, and ensuring that differentiation is in the outcome of the activity.

2   **Accept innovation and individuality,** even if the solutions pupils deliver from your task-briefings are not what you had in (your) mind.

3   If work is technically poor or if the presentation is weak, **react positively to the ideas and thoughts behind it** and help pupils to develop skills in self-expression.

4   **Ask open-ended questions and accept a range of answers.** Try to avoid asking questions to which you anticipate only one 'right' answer (unless you are dealing with matters of fact).

5   **Allow time for pupils to experiment, make mistakes and explore ideas.** When presenting pupils with a new area of work, new techniques or materials, give them a chance to explore possibilities and try things out before you launch into a major piece of work.

6   **Encourage the use of rough-work books.** Pupils may often feel it is easier to be creative in rough-books, and you can then help them redraft their original ideas in work where presentation is given their attention.

7   **Use brainstorming** with individuals, in small groups or as a whole class. Remind pupils that in brainstorming sessions, all ideas are valued and none criticized.

8 **Try to set open-ended tasks that encourage divergent rather than convergent outcomes.** This will not only be more interesting for your pupils, but also for you.

9 **Get pupils to work in groups on a range of ideas.** Don't ask them to pick the best of these, but ask them to find ways to incorporate the best elements of all of the contributions produced in the groups.

10 **Ask pupils to think about 'dream' and 'nightmare' solutions to problems.** 'What would this be like if everything went in the best possible way?' 'Now what would it be like if everything went wrong?' Help pupils to distil learning points from these activities and the scenarios they think of.

35

Helping pupils to write essays

In many formal examinations, pupils are required to put what they know into the form of written essays. In coursework too, pupils' skills at writing essays may count for a lot. The following suggestions may help you to help them to approach this task successfully and effectively.

1   **Help pupils to plan essays.** Show them ways of mapping out the ideas they may subsequently turn into paragraphs in their final versions of an essay.

2   **Remind pupils to look carefully at the title or briefing.** We all know how easy it is to stray away from the main topic, and to end up writing things which (however interesting) are irrelevant to the task in progress.

3   **Help pupils to analyse what is required.** Remind them of the significance of such key words as 'how', 'why', 'when', 'where', and so on in essay briefings. In particular, alert pupils to what they should try to do when asked to 'compare' or 'contrast' or both.

4   **Remind pupils that it takes several drafts to write a good essay.** Encourage them to get their ideas down on paper, and then spend some time rearranging them before they come up with their 'final essay'.

5   **Help pupils to see the importance of firm conclusions.** Any essay usually requires the writer to come to some sort of conclusion – or at least to sum up what has been said. It is important that essays don't just stop in full flow, but arrive at a decisive ending.

6   **Help pupils to make good introductions.** There is no better time to compose the introduction that when we know exactly what we're introducing! Suggest to pupils that they should write the introductions to their essays quite late, when they know exactly what their essays will have covered.

7   **Remind pupils of the usefulness of practice.** The best way to become better at writing essays is to write lots of them. Or better still, to plan lots of them – it is possible to plan several essays in the time it takes to put one together.

8   **Quantity is not the same as quality.** Remind pupils that it's not a matter of writing a lot, rather a matter of good quality writing that counts.

9   **Get pupils to mark essays for themselves.** Sometimes, the best way to alert pupils to the strengths and weaknesses in essay-writing is to help them to allocate marks to examples of essays.

10   **Give pupils the chance to compose an essay as a group.** This can help individual pupils to learn from each other. It can also allow any criticisms to be shared by the group, rather than received by individual pupils.

Part 5 Providing Personal and Pastoral Care

36

Being an effective form tutor

This can be one of the most rewarding of all the aspects of the work of a secondary school teacher. You can really get to know your pupils as individuals and they will relate to you on a much more human level than they may do to their subject teachers. Schools vary in the amount of emphasis given to the pastoral role of the form tutor but in most cases you will be expected to get to know your group very well and follow their progress on every level.

1 **Get to know your form as individuals.** Learn their names as quickly as you can. Talk to some pupils each day about some aspect of their school or home life. Try not to talk always to the approachable members of the class. Make an effort to involve all the group in activities.

2 **Build a collection of 'portraits' of the pupils in your form.** This can be done with the pupils themselves, for example containing details of their hobbies, favourite foods, best-liked music, sports achievements, and so on. Try to build up a way of finding out what makes each individual 'tick'.

3 **Be an ally, as well as a teacher.** Make it clear to pupils in your form that you are there to help them. This in turn means that you expect them to tell you when they need your help. Be ready to be their principal contact if they need to share personal or family problems that could be affecting their lives.

4 **Praise good social behaviour.** While such behaviour affects all teachers and pupils, it is often left to the form tutor to be the monitor of general attitudes and demeanour. Invoke 'team spirit' and a feel of belonging – the 'we are the best class' feeling.

5 **Be approachable** – leave time to talk to your class – don't always be preoccupied with administrative tasks or preparing the next lesson.

6 **Be a troubleshooter!** Offer to help 'smooth the waves' when pupils in your form get into difficulties with your colleagues. You will often be able to explain to your colleagues difficulties that the particular pupils are going through, that they could not otherwise have known about.

7 **In form base time, set small tasks which will get pupils working together in different configurations.** This helps to avoid the class becoming polarized into cliques that always work together.

8 **Encourage pride in the form base classroom where feasible.** Providing (or encouraging pupils to provide) posters and plants can help make a form classroom special to the form.

9 **Pay attention to small details.** Some pupils like it when you remember their birthdays or if you comment on their contributions to school exhibitions, performances or sports event achievements.

10 **Recognize individual differences:** you can treat pupils equally without treating them identically. Try to ensure that both genders get equal amounts of time and attention, but don't ignore quiet pupils just because they are no bother.

37

Getting pupils to talk to you

When pupils are talking to you, you have their undivided attention. The more you can get them to do the talking, the more learning they will achieve.

1 **Invite questions from individual pupils by name.** Give them the chance to explain more about their questions, so that everyone becomes interested in the answers.

2 **Make full use of the questions pupils ask.** Ask the class if anyone is willing or able to answer a question which a pupil has asked. Give volunteers every encouragement to answer.

3 **Don't 'put down' incorrect answers from pupils.** Gently confirm that the answers are not yet quite correct, and invite further replies from any pupils who have further ideas.

4 **Ask questions in an interesting way.** Make it appear that you really don't yet know what the answers may be. Draw the answers out of pupils, by asking them leading questions, which help them to arrive at sensible answers.

5 **Encourage pupils to contribute their own questions.** Help pupils themselves to think of the questions that the class needs to address. If the class 'owns' the questions, more pupils will be interested in the answers to them.

6 **Be available as an expert witness.** Arrange one-to-one times, where any pupil can come to you, and ask you anything, or tell you anything. Use what they ask or tell you as an agenda for future class discussions or activities.

7 **Be someone who can find someone who knows.** Make it clear to pupils that they can ask you (or tell you) about anything at all, but that you can't be expected to know all the answers – but you can find someone who does.

8 **Let pupils in to selected parts of your world.** Talk to classes about 'shareable' things in your own life from time to time, to help the pupils appreciate that you too have feelings and emotions. But handle personal anecdotes with care; it's easy to become boring.

9 **Accept silly questions.** When pupils ask 'silly' questions, or say 'silly' things, treat them as perfectly reasonable questions or comments, encouraging other pupils to ask questions or make comments.

10 **Bring everyone in.** Identify those pupils who don't ask questions or give comments, and try to draw them into discussions, for example by giving them the responsibility for taking charge of a group discussion of a matter arising from a question that has already been asked.

38

Helping pupils who don't believe in themselves

Personal self-esteem is important for everyone (including ourselves). Human nature being what it is, there will always be a proportion of pupils who (sometimes for very complex reasons) underestimate themselves. Don't think that you can solve the world's problems by yourself! You'll have too many of your own at first. You may wish to concentrate on teaching and surviving yourself in the early stages! However, some suggestions on how to help pupils with low self-esteem are given below.

1 **Capitalize on their successes.** Remind yourself about how self-belief usually comes through success. Try to ensure that pupils who have a self-esteem problem are given things to do in which they will demonstrably succeed. It can help to break something up into more manageable tasks where such pupils can succeed, before going on to the next stage.

2 **Be aware of sensitivity when giving feedback.** Take particular care when giving feedback to pupils who may be sensitive because of a self-esteem problem. Avoid the use of any negative 'final language', including such words as 'not satisfactory', or 'wrong'.

3 **Help pupils identify their strengths.** Help pupils who are feeling low on self-esteem by reminding them about things that you already know they are good at, and where you can point to evidence which convinces them of their achievements.

4 **Help pupils accept their weaknesses.** Encourage pupils to regard weaknesses as not-yet-developed strengths. Help them to believe that the fact that they can't *yet* do a thing does not mean they can never do it.

5 **Show that weaknesses are really opportunities to grow.** Suggest that pupils regard weaknesses as opportunities rather than threats. Show them that being aware of a weakness is in itself a strength, and a cause for positive self-esteem.

6 **Suggest that low self-esteem is part of anyone's normal life at times.** Remind pupils that most people go through periods of low self-esteem as a perfectly normal and natural part of growing up and developing. Where possible, give illustrations of your own feelings and approaches during such times.

7 **Help pupils find out what makes them tick.** Do a group exercise with pupils, asking 'What sorts of things make you feel good about yourself?' Several pupils may discover positive factors about themselves that they had not consciously thought of before.

8 **Help pupils to share feelings.** Encourage pupils to go public with (at least some of) their feelings. This will need handling with sensitivity and tact. For example, have a 'feelings washing-line' at the side of a classroom, where pupils can peg a piece of paper saying how they feel today and why.

9 **Devise tasks where pupils will succeed.** Have a stock of small useful tasks you can give out to pupils who need a boost in their self-esteem – tasks which you know they can succeed at, and which will be seen by others to have been useful and successful.

10 **Don't forget your own feelings.** Monitor your own self-esteem, and the contributing factors and circumstances. We never stop learning about how our own minds and emotions function.

39

Coping with emotional pupils

Human beings are an emotional species. By the time we become teachers, we've had a fair amount of experience at handling our own emotions. Pupils, however, will continue to meet emotions quite new to them. The following are some of the ways we can help them.

1 **Accept the emotion** – don't try to persuade pupils to 'pull yourself together now!' There may be times when pupils have so much on their minds because of outside circumstances that they are not able to learn. Be sensitive to this and reduce the pressure or discover if they can be helped through it.

2 **Find out what's behind the emotion.** Gently and carefully gather information on the cause of strong emotions. The first explanations of the cause are often far from the real cause. Yawning and lack of concentration may sometimes be outward signs of inward confusion and distress, not boredom with what you are teaching.

3 **Help pupils to put it in their own words.** Encourage pupils to explain how they feel, and why they feel that way. Use questions which help to draw out their feelings, without making judgemental replies at an early stage.

4 **Avoid alienating pupils affected by emotion.** Try to avoid the isolation of any pupil experiencing a strong emotion. Help them to feel that emotions are a perfectly normal part of life, and that there is no shame or weakness involved in having emotions.

5 **Help pupils to identify the source of their emotions.** When the emotion concerned is anger, help pupils to clarify the exact causes of such a feeling. Often, once the causes have been expressed to someone else, the feeling is considerably relieved.

6 **Help pupils see that emotions are natural.** Openly discuss at 'normal' times the human nature of having emotions and feelings. Explain to pupils how the first time they experience particular emotions and feelings, they can feel quite out of their depth, but that subsequent experience helps them develop their own coping strategies.

7 **Don't go it alone.** Don't expect to be able to deal with all emotional situations on your own. Find out which colleagues are particularly good at dealing with such situations, and bring them in when possible to help you.

8 **Bring in the experts when necessary.** Be on the lookout for emotional problems which will benefit from expert help. When following up such expertise, be careful that no feelings of stigma arise. It is often the sensitive and intelligent mind that ties itself in knots temporarily due to over-emotion.

9 **Minimize feelings of weakness.** Do anything you can to minimize the feeling of an over-emotional pupil of 'being different'. Feelings of alienation are often the most distressing part of an emotional episode.

10 **Show that you too are human.** When it is useful, share your own emotions and feelings, and your own ways of coping with swings of mood. Use your judgement to decide which parts of your own experience can be useful for your pupils to learn from.

40

Breaking bad news

Sadly, bad news has to be broken by someone, and that sometimes means us! There is no substitute for a course in counselling, but the following suggestions may provide some ideas about how to break bad news to pupils.

1 **Be sure of your facts.** Make sure you know exactly what the bad news is, and where the information came from. Have contact telephone numbers written down.

2 **Don't do it alone.** If possible, enlist the help of a colleague before you start the difficult task of breaking bad news to a pupil – preferably, a colleague of the opposite sex to yourself.

3 **Prepare the way** – find a suitable location which is private but informal (breaking some bad news in front of a whole class could be very traumatic for the recipient of the news).

4 **Be ready for the next steps.** Plan in advance what will be done after breaking the news (for example who will take the pupil to the hospital, or home).

5 **Avoid highlighting bad news.** Call the pupil concerned out of the class as innocently as possible (for example 'Sorry, but could we go along to Mrs Roger's room where I believe she has a message for you?').

6 **Proceed gently.** If possible, invite the pupil to sit down first. Only then say something along the lines 'I'm sorry, but I've got some rather bad news for you', then deliver the news as gently as possible, giving what comfort you can as needed.

7 **Accept emotional reactions.** If the news results in tears, it is usually best to encourage: 'that's all right now, let it all out', rather than say 'pull yourself together!' Particularly when you have a colleague present, one or other of you can hold a hand or give a hug as appropriate.

8 **Inform other people with due care.** It may be necessary to tell the rest of the class about the bad news. However, it's important not to break confidences at this stage. For example, it's better to tell them that 'Sheila has had some sad news which will have given her a bit of a shock', rather than to say 'Sheila's mother has been injured in an accident'.

9 **Decide who needs to know what.** Depending on the nature of the news, decide whether all of your colleagues need to be alerted to the details, or just the fact that the pupil concerned needs to be treated with particular sensitivity during the time to come.

10 **Keep track of events.** It can make a big difference if you can continue to monitor the situation. This may mean maintaining contact with the pupil or the family, in which case it is important that one person does this rather than too many callers or enquirers.

41

Helping pupils to recover from setbacks

Circumstances overtake all of us sometimes. Pupils may lose a fortnight due to illness, or have setbacks in their family lives which knock them out of their stride. Also, pupils often need help in recovering from failure. The following suggestions may help you to help them to regain their momentum.

1 **Assemble your first-aid kit.** Build up your own collection of handouts and resources covering key topics in your teaching, which you can issue to pupils. This can assist you to help pupils make up for lost time when necessary.

2 **Encourage pupils to ask.** Encourage pupils who have missed key lessons on important topics to make lists of questions about things they can't understand as they work on catching up. Make time to be available to respond to these questions.

3 **Encourage peer-group support.** Help pupils who have missed something to use their classmates as a resource to help them catch up. Explain to the whole class how useful it is to explain a topic to someone.

4 **Don't look back yet!** Suggest to pupils who have fallen behind that it is more important to keep up with what is going on at present than to try and do all the catching up overnight. Encourage them to catch up a bit at a time, while keeping up with the rest of the class on current topics as well.

5 **Have other ways of catching up ready.** For particularly crucial parts of your course, have alternative learning pathways readily available for any pupils who miss key lessons. For example, turn these parts into small learning packages or interactive handouts, which pupils can work through in their own time. Also, run 'repeat' (rather than 'remedial') sessions on these key topics, for anyone who did not 'get it' first time around.

6   **Help pupils not to panic.** Help pupils who have missed something important to keep it in perspective. It may seem like a mountain at the time, but once understood, the problem will quickly be forgotten.

7   **Encourage pupils to regard 'failure' as a useful stage towards success.** Remind them that they themselves are not failures; it is simply that they have not yet succeeded at the particular task involved.

8   **Acknowledge the value of making mistakes.** Give pupils examples of how 'getting it wrong at first' is one of the most natural ways to learn things successfully.

9   **Help pupils look at their tactics.** Where pupils are preparing for a resit exam, encourage them not only to explore the parts that caused them problems before, but also to analyse the ways they went about preparing for the exam and sitting it. Indeed, advise pupils that a past failure can be a distinct advantage when it comes to the next occasion.

10   **Tell them about Edison,** whose 100th attempt to make an electric light-bulb was successful. He dismissed the rest as '99 ways *not* to try to make a light-bulb'.

42

Helping pupils towards university or employment

Sometimes it is thought that the 'careers adviser' bears all the responsibility for pupils' future progress. However, pupils need all the guidance and support we can all give them in addition to specialist advice. The following suggestions may help you to support your own pupils.

1 **Help pupils make their own resources.** Ask pupils to prepare a 'curriculum vitae' as an assessed task. Give them feedback on the ways that their c.vs may be viewed by admission tutors in universities, or by prospective employers.

2 **Help pupils fly their own kites.** Help pupils to identify strengths in their own experience, which are worth showing clearly when they apply for employment or further education.

3 **Show pupils what counts.** Alert pupils to the things that look 'good' on applications. In particular, extol the virtues of things that show pupils' responsibility, cooperativeness and initiative.

4 **Coach pupils in the art of 'interview technique'.** Use class role-play exercises to help pupils familiarize themselves with the processes of interviews.

5 **Give pupils safe 'dry-runs'.** If possible, engage pupils in making videos of simulated interviews. Remember that the act of capturing an interview on video automatically develops quite acute observation of the processes involved.

6 **Help pupils to see what's being sought.** Use case-studies to alert pupils to what prospective interviewers may be looking for. For example, show pupils a video of three different interviews for a job, and ask them to list the respective merits and weaknesses of the candidates, and to select the best candidate.

7   **Let pupils taste further opportunities.** Take advantage of open days at local colleges or universities, to give pupils a taste of what it would be like to continue their education there.

8   **Help pupils to see what has already succeeded.** Invite past pupils who gained employment or went on to college back to the school to share their experience with pupils.

9   **Help pupils find out what they need to be able to do.** Set groups of pupils the task of drawing up an advertisement for a job, spelling out the duties involved in the job, and identifying the experience that is being sought in candidates.

10   **Practice makes perfect.** Remind pupils that becoming good at interviews is best achieved by practice, and that one 'bad' interview should not put them off. Encourage them to learn even more from unsuccessful interviews than from successful ones.

43

Coping with parents' evenings

These occasions can prove quite an ordeal at the end of a busy day – especially if you're not well prepared. In some subject areas you could come into contact with 250 different pupils each week, so if you can get into the habit of writing brief notes about pupils' progress as it happens you will find interviews with parents much less worrying. Parents' evenings are not the place to discuss major issues, and if possible you should let parents know in advance if there are serious matters which may need lengthier or more private discussions. As a general rule, there should be no major surprises in store for parents.

1 Talk to your pupils in advance to **establish which parents will be attending.** Discuss with the pupils what they feel their successes and failures have been so far in the course.

2 **Make it clear to parents who you are.** This is particularly important when parents' evenings are held in a large space such as the school hall. Have a large card on your table, with your name on it and the subject you teach, or the form you are responsible for.

3 **Make sure you know who the pupils are!** If it is too early in the term to have learnt all their names, ensure that you check out your notes and marks when the class is present during lessons beforehand. It can help to make very brief notes about individual achievements or characteristics in your mark book as you become aware of them. This will be an invaluable aid to writing reports about them later in the term.

4 **Take along some examples of the pupils' work where appropriate.** Parents are very interested not only in their own child's progress but also in the type of work done in lessons.

5 **Make brief notes of which parents talk to you, and the main points of discussion.** You will often want to follow up particular things arising from the discussion later.

6   **Avoid odious comparisons.** Talk about the pupil under consideration, rather than their classmates or siblings.

7   **Look after yourself:** try to arrange for a hot drink to be brought to you, or at least have in reserve mineral water and mints. These evenings can be very long.

8   **Concentrate on pupils' behaviour and achievements rather than personality;** parents may be more amenable to criticisms of what their children are actually doing rather than their children's personality traits (which may be inherited!).

9   **Avoid the temptation to get drawn into discussions of the shortcomings of other members of staff.** However justified and satisfying this may sometimes be, it is not terribly professional!

10   **Try not to speed up towards the end!** You may be tired, but parents may well have been waiting a long time to see you and they deserve just as much of your attention as those you saw at the beginning of the evening.

44

Dealing with difficult parents

'Difficult' parents are usually ones who come to complain! The best advice to offer is not to deal directly with difficult parents – but get someone who is paid to do that sort of job to handle it. This does not always work out so easily in practice. The following suggestions may help you when it falls to you to sort out a difficult situation. The first two suggestions are evasion tactics – but you'll need the rest sooner or later too!

1 **Refer the complaint to your head of department** or a senior member of staff and if possible get them to deal with it without involving you in face-to-face contact with the parents. (Perhaps you should also pass on to your senior colleague a copy of this list!)

2 **If you have made a mistake, admit it** to your head of department or head teacher and let them sort it out on your behalf.

3 **Develop your listening skills!** The cause of many difficult encounters is that parents don't feel we are letting them tell us what is concerning them. It is all too easy to jump in far too early to try to defend ourselves. Let them have their full say – indeed draw their concerns from them. Then prepare to reply.

4 **Think of difficulties in terms of situations and actions, rather than people.** Explain to parents (and pupils) that it has nothing to do with particular personalities, but is a matter of events, consequences and effects.

5 **Avoid difficulties 'spilling over'.** When you have had a difficulty with a pupil (or a parent) over one matter, make it clear that this does not cause you to bear a grudge, and that you are treating every new situation as a fresh start.

6 Before you discuss any matters concerning their child with parents **make sure that you are clear in your own mind of the reasons for your actions and behaviour.** If they can see your point of view, they are likely to become less difficult.

7 **Stay calm, don't get drawn into arguments.** Repeat your own version of events and justify it in a professional manner. Avoid confrontation – know when you can back down discreetly and when it is important not to do so. When you suspect that there could be major difficulties, ensure that you don't see parents completely on your own.

8 **Be prepared to understand, even when you don't agree.** Often, difficulties can be caused when parents can't see that you understand their point of view. If you can convince them that you do indeed understand, but in your professional capacity can't agree with them, they may become more ready to listen to your own point of view.

9 **Be the first to rebuild bridges.** This sometimes goes against human nature, but we teachers as professional people are often better able to reopen channels of communication after a difficulty.

10 **Use encounters with difficult parents as a learning opportunity.** Painful as it may be at the time, we can build up a lot of experience by learning from each encounter, and asking ourselves 'What would I do differently if a similar situation arose tomorrow?'

45

Coping with emergencies

We can forgive ourselves for having nightmares about emergencies and how we may cope with them! However, an important part of the learning experience of our pupils is seeing how we cope with the unexpected. The following suggestions may help you rise to the occasion when necessary.

1 **Look positively at emergencies.** Remind yourself that each emergency you are faced with is a productive learning experience, and that next time a similar situation arises, you will have your additional experience to help you out.

2 **Be prepared.** Anticipate as many emergencies as it is reasonable to expect. For example, get some training in first aid. Being that bit more confident can make a lot of difference to how you feel when coping with a crisis.

3 **Expect the unexpected!** 'Emergencies' are by definition 'the unexpected'. Take positive steps to be alert to early-warning signals, so that nothing is really unexpected.

4 **Know someone who's good at dealing with the unexpected.** Build your own support network of people who are good at handling difficult or stressful situations. Learn from them, observing their coping strategies.

5 **Don't try to do all the coping on your own.** Some of the pupils may be able to do useful things to help you to focus your own efforts on the most critical parts of the actions needed to handle an emergency.

6 **Move the emergency.** When possible, take the emergency to a less public place. A quiet corner of an empty classroom may be better territory to sort out an emergency than in front of a whole class.

7 **No one can handle all emergencies first time.** Don't imagine that you are required to cope with distinction with each and every emergency you ever meet. When things don't work out, don't dwell on feelings of failure, but rather extract what you can learn from the situation, then let it go.

8 **Collect case lore.** With colleagues, build up a collection of case-study notes on emergencies and how they were handled. Learn from things that succeeded in the past, and also from things that could have been handled more successfully with hindsight.

9 **Be ready to act.** Be as prepared as you can. For example, have quick access to pupils' home addresses and telephone numbers, and ensure that you keep your personal datafile updated and close to hand.

10 **Don't panic!** Being seen to panic helps no one. Try to appear calm and collected even when your mind is in a whirl! Remind yourself that emergencies are usually over in a very short time – it only *seems* like a century.

Part 6 Being an Effective Colleague

46

Working with colleagues

It can be lonely at the chalkface! Yet it does often carry the comfort of privacy. However, with cross-curriculum developments and initiatives, it is becoming increasingly important for teachers to be able to work together effectively and constructively. There are many benefits to be realised from collaborative working, not least the fact that colleagues can take over from us at short notice when necessary. It also helps to feel you have friends and allies when the going gets tough. The following suggestions may help you to take advantage of such benefits.

1 **Collaborate with colleagues.** Co-produce teaching and learning materials with colleagues as much as possible to produce co-ownership of resources. The quality and effectiveness of resources produced by more than one teacher is much higher than we could have produced on our own (your three co-authors have found this in writing this book together!).

2 **Keep colleagues well informed.** Brief colleagues working with you carefully, especially any part-time colleagues or temporary teachers who could not be with you during planning discussions for the courses you're teaching. Keep colleagues informed about how your own work is going too.

3 **Plan how you will work jointly.** Plan and organize your collaborative work well in advance, for example using flowcharts to show how your roles will integrate.

4 **Plan to be able to cover for each other.** Develop your ability to provide emergency backup for other colleagues to cope with contingencies. Help to enable colleagues to take over from you at short notice when necessary too.

5 **All work and no play?** Take full advantage of social opportunities to get to know colleagues informally, so you can enjoy each other's company out of the context of your work as well as in school.

6 **Don't be seen to disagree!** Ensure that when your views or opinions differ from those of colleagues, you avoid arguing in the presence of pupils! And if you are new to teaching, don't forget you may have a lot to learn from older hands.

7 **Keep to deadlines.** Meet deadlines for collaborative tasks when colleagues are relying on your keeping to schedules on time. Attend meetings promptly and properly prepared.

8 **Share your own resources and skills.** Make available to colleagues your teaching materials, including overheads, handouts and exercises. Invite colleagues to observe or participate in some of your lessons, and ask for their comments about how the sessions went. Similarly, respond to colleagues' invitations or requests to sit in on their lessons, and give them feedback kindly and supportively when they request it.

9 **Be willing to ask for help.** Seek advice and suggestions from colleagues (even when you don't need it) and make your colleagues feel valued and respected for their help.

10 **Monitor collaborative working.** Promote the benefits of team teaching to colleagues, and help them start to work in teams. Take time to review openly the processes by which you work together, and improve and develop these processes whenever you can.

47

Coping with difficult heads of department or senior staff

If you are finding one of your superiors difficult to deal with, the chances are you are not the only one. Find an ally and discuss the problem in confidence – it will give you the strength to carry on!

1 **Be careful to distinguish between conflicts of ideas and conflicts of personality.** It is possible to work with people in either situation, but easier to manage when you know exactly what sorts of conflict are involved.

2 **Refrain from inappropriately aggressive behaviour in conflict situations.** This includes consciously refraining from sarcasm, cynical remarks and bursts of temper.

3 **Find out what other colleagues think too.** Get other colleagues to witness your achievements, as well as your boss. Enlist the support of others in your department and work together as a team.

4 **Avoid letting previous differences of opinion colour current interactions.** It is possible to agree on present issues even when you've already disagreed on past matters.

5 **Value other people's opinions, even when they are the opposite of your own.** You can disagree completely with what someone thinks about an issue, without taking away their right to have their own views.

6 **Avoid the temptation to undermine the professional dignity or self-esteem of 'difficult' senior colleagues.** They will usually be in a position to return such actions doubly!

7 **Check that you are indeed trying to do what senior colleagues ask you to do.** Make a note of what you have been asked to do and check this with a senior teacher before and after completion.

8   **Identify the exact nature of a difficulty.** Talk about it to senior members of staff on a professional level, ensuring that others understand your situation. Try to develop a simple action-plan to help you overcome the difficulty.

9   **Cover yourself.** Ensure that difficulties are placed on the agenda for department meetings, and that decisions are minuted – offer to take the minutes yourself if necessary.

10 **Accept that it's not easy being the boss!** There may be all kinds of pressures, of which you are quite unaware, on your Head of Department.

48

Managing a department

Although you may not yet be in the position of head of department, it is useful to be aware of the issues involved in such responsibilities, and the difficulties that might arise. Of course, if you're brave enough, you may decide to copy the suggestions below to your head of department.

1 **Hold regular meetings with staff, which are timetabled in advance.** This ensures that everyone is ready to attend, even if there is little on the agenda. You can always cancel a meeting if there is nothing to discuss, but it is sometimes difficult to get colleagues together at short notice when there is something important to decide. Regular meetings, even if only brief, ease communication and foster a sense of belonging to a team.

2 **Meetings should always have an agenda and be minuted.** Don't prolong meetings unnecessarily – prioritize items of business and set time limits for discussion if there is a lot on the agenda. Adopt the philosophy that a well-chaired one-hour meeting can always cover as much ground as a half-day meeting that is allowed to drift!

3 **Get members of the department to take the minutes in rotation**. The act of minuting a meeting helps people to distance themselves at least temporarily from their own personal points of view, and overall helps to keep things in perspective.

4 **Make the outcomes of meetings definite and accessible.** Ensure that things which must be done are put in writing and accompanied by a completion date, and that all colleagues receive copies.

5 **Delegate areas of responsibility fairly within the department.** Ensure that new or inexperienced colleagues also take some area of responsibility, however small.

6 **Ensure that all staff feel valued and involved.** Involve all colleagues in discussions of the allocation of capitation, and in budgeting and ordering of stock.

7 **Adopt a team approach to planning.** Get colleagues to work together to develop policies so that all are involved at every stage. When everyone in the department has a sense of ownership of plans and policies, there is much more certainty that the plans will come to fruition smoothly and quickly.

8 **Keep everyone fully informed, but minimize paperwork.** Avoid excessive use of circulated papers and memoranda. These may move swiftly from pigeonhole to wastepaper basket! Use a notice board which all can access to aid communication. Have space on the board for individual colleagues to post replies or reactions to decisions, so that all views can be shared.

9 **Plan social as well as business meetings for the department.** When people are friends as well as colleagues, a department runs happily.

10 **Acknowledge difficult decisions.** When a decision needs to be taken on a matter where there are different opinions, facilitate a group session where staff can express the strengths and weaknesses they see in various alternative approaches to the decision to be made. If there is no clear outcome, agree on a trial approach, with a review date when the matter will be discussed on the basis of experience of the trial.

49

Covering for absent colleagues

'Oh but I'm indispensable!' wouldn't we all like to think? The fact is that now and again someone is going to have to take over for us, and sometimes at very short notice indeed. Similarly, we need to be able to cover for absent colleagues. The following suggestions may help you to make your 'guest appearances' successful – and less stressful for you.

1 **If possible get an oral briefing in advance.** When colleagues are taking planned absence, this helps so that you can clarify exactly what you are required to do.

2 **Try to have available an assortment of activities for all ages and abilities.** This can prove invaluable when you are left in the lurch without work set for pupils to do. Such activities might include crosswords, wordsearches, reading tasks, puzzles and discussion topics.

3 **Carry with you an emergency pack of paper, ballpoint pens and so on, for pupils to use.** Absent teachers often have the set of exercise books at home with them, especially if it is an unexpected absence.

4 **Don't expect to be able to learn names in a one-off substitution class.** However it may be helpful to draw a sketch plan of the desk positions and pass it round at the beginning of the class, asking pupils to write in their names (legibly). This may help you to identify pupils and to have a class register (but be aware that some might take the mickey out of you by substituting false names!).

5 **Don't allow yourself to get drawn into discussions about how much better you are than their normal teacher!** This may be flattering, but doesn't engender a professional and collegial approach.

6 **Don't be overambitious about what you can achieve.** Especially with a one-off substitution, be realistic about what you are likely to be able to do as a relative stranger to the pupils.

7 **Don't stand for any nonsense.** Use all the techniques in your repertoire to settle pupils down and maintain order. Remember that pupils will often try to give cover teachers a hard time!

8 **Don't be surprised if pupils are angry or resentful about your covering their class.** Some pupils hate change, and you may be replacing their favourite teacher.

9 **Keep your sense of humour.** This may be difficult in trying circumstances, but do your best!

10 **Be considerate to the absent teacher.** Ensure that pupils leave the room tidy, and count in all materials used. Coming back to depleted stock after an illness or emergency is not encouraging!

50

Coping with stress

Our job can be a stressful one. In addition, there are episodes of stress in most people's lives at one time or another. The following suggestions may help you to handle stressful times.

1 **Accept that stress is a natural part of human life,** and that it does not help at all simply to allocate blame for our feelings of stress, or to rail against the situation.

2 **Regard stress as useful!** Try to develop the attitude that every stressful situation can be viewed as a useful developmental experience. Learning to cope with stress, or even 'going under' temporarily, can both be used to build up coping strategies.

3 **Monitor your stress levels.** Keep track of whether you are stressed or not – you may not realise it when you are in fact stressed. Other people can often tell us about our stress levels – provided we give them the chance and don't shout them down!

4 **Decide when stress needs some action.** Accept that a certain amount of stress is actually healthy, raising our adrenalin levels and creative thinking capacities. The time to worry about stress is when it gets in the way of a balanced, enjoyable life, or affects people around us.

5 **Be aware of the symptoms of stress.** Remember that when we are stressed, we can easily magnify small irritations out of all proportion. If you find yourself over-reacting to everyday things that pupils do, don't blame them.

6 **Build up your own support network,** including family, friends, colleagues and even relative strangers. Getting away from a stressful situation for a while can help us to recharge our batteries and return better able to handle that situation.

7   **Exchange with colleagues and friends strategies for coping with stress.** It is most productive to do this at a time when you feel quite unstressed, as you can then look at the various coping strategies calmly and objectively.

8   **It's up to us how we react to stress.** Common as it is for other people to get the blame for our stress, there's little anyone can do to alter how other people are, or how they behave. It is our task to readjust our reactions to stressful situations.

9   **Many kinds of stress are completely avoidable** – for example the stress felt when we're late, unprepared, or over-extended. But remember, it is sometimes possible to avoid such situations simply by saying 'No!'

10   **Don't cross too many bridges!** One of the biggest stress factors we have to cope with is the possibility of failure or rejection. It is human nature to worry about many things that simply don't ever happen. Save your mental energies for handling the few things that need your coping strategies.

(That was our 500th tip! Here are a few more.)

51

Planning your career progression

When you start out in teaching it may seem a miracle to you that you have managed to survive your first year without having a nervous breakdown or getting the sack! It can, however, be surprising how soon the opportunity may come up to develop your skills and further your career. INSET (In-Service Education and Training) opportunities can play a vital part in extending the range of teaching that you can handle well.

1   **Attend INSET wherever possible,** if at all relevant to your work. You could end up as the only person around with some specialist knowledge. The more things you know at least a bit about, the greater your employability.

2   **The best way to learn is to try to teach!** Make the most of every opportunity to run INSET workshops or discussions within your department or school in your own specialist area. However, if you are new to teaching, don't try to teach any grandparent to suck eggs!

3   **Keep yourself informed.** Take an interest in wider educational issues; read the educational press and attend professional association meetings.

4   **Set yourself clear goals** – even if they seem unrealistic to start with. Where do you want to be in five years' time, and what would it take to get you there? Use the appraisal process to help you clarify and plan your personal and professional development.

5   **Cultivate your profile.** Make sure that people know what you are doing in the classroom, and if you are involved in any initiatives, pilot schemes and developments.

6   **Involve yourself in extra-curricular activities.** Use your outside interests and hobbies to extend your contribution to the full range of things that the school offers pupils and staff.

7   **Take opportunities to work-shadow other colleagues.** One of the most productive ways of improving one's own teaching is to see how other people do it well – and better still, how they do it badly!

8   **Build up your own network.** Take every opportunity to make contacts with teachers involved in your subject in other schools. Exchange ideas, and teaching and learning resources with them.

9   **Keep on studying.** Always be on the lookout for ways you can extend the subject range which one day you may wish to teach.

10 **Build up your own teaching portfolio.** Keep a collection of things you have designed, reflections on new ideas you have tried out. Such a portfolio can be very valuable when it comes to appraisal interviews, or interviews for promotion or new posts elsewhere. It's often a good idea to keep a collection of photographs of activities and events you've organized or planned which might otherwise be difficult to document.

52

Applying for jobs

In most professions, including teaching, advancement nowadays more often seems to come through moving on than by staying put. The following suggestions may help you move on when you want to.

1 **Keep up your curriculum vitae as an on-going task** – preferably on computer disk. It is extremely useful to be able to print off an updated copy at short notice, when an interesting opportunity seems worth applying for.

2 **Make your cv read interestingly** – not just a catalogue of all the things you've done in your career.

3 **Get your wording right.** Take care in working out the wording you will use in a convincing letter of application for a post. Make such letters specific to the school and the post that you are applying for, and include indications of how you personally would approach taking on the post.

4 **Keep up appearances.** Remember how important the appearance of a completed application form can be. It is often difficult to type information into boxes on printed forms, so decide whether to engage a skilled typist, or to practise yourself on photocopies of the form until you can get it just right.

5 **Know what you said to whom.** Especially when you may have several applications in progress at one time, it is essential to keep photocopies of exactly what you said in each particular instance. The exact words you used make ideal reading while preparing for any interview you're called to – it is the self-same words which are being read by the interview panel.

6 **Remember the importance of face-to-face communication skills.** If you are to convince other people at interviews, these skills will be valuable to you.

7 **Be prepared for open-ended questions.** Often, at an interview you will be asked to 'tell us a bit about yourself'. Such questions can be harder to handle than direct questions about your experience. Practise giving (say) a three-minute summary of your career to date, focusing on your successes rather than any difficulties you've met.

8 **All interviews are useful experiences – even the painful ones.** Regard each interview not as the one-and-only opportunity to the job of your dreams, but as a useful chance to develop and improve your approach in the future. It's often when you don't particularly want the job in question that you're offered the most interesting options!

9 **Practice helps a lot!** If you can make the opportunity, practise your interview technique with friends or colleagues. It's good for any of us to become used to the sound of our own voices answering questions and talking about our aims and ambitions.

10 **Don't let your technique go rusty!** Apply for new jobs regularly, even when you're perfectly satisfied with your present post. It is always useful experience to take stock of your career to date, and it is often valuable to show your colleagues that you're not necessarily content with your present status. 'Nothing ventured, nothing gained' is a useful motto!

Conclusion

Teaching is a rewarding career but it can be demanding and frustrating, as well as enormously draining of energy. It is one in which we never stop learning, not only from what goes well but also from mishaps and disasters. Even very experienced teachers sometimes feel we need some encouragement and support to stop us going stale.

The hints and suggestions we describe here aim to provide trained and trainee teachers with a few extra ideas that might help along the way. We offer them in the spirit of things that we wished someone had told us when we first started out, as they could have saved us quite a lot of work and worry, as well as ensuring that our pupils got a better deal out of us too.

We hope you have found this useful; if you have, we would be delighted to hear from you, as it makes us feel happy! Similarly, if you feel we have omitted important areas, missed the point or got things wrong in places, please let us know. We depend on feedback to enable us continuously to improve our writing. You can contact us via our publishers.

Sally Brown
Carolyn Earlam
Phil Race

Index